theoutsidetable

photography véronique cornille   Food and flavours of the Nelson region

remember, experience, dream

art

The Suter
Te Aratoi o Whakatu

The Bishop Suter Art Gallery Te Aratoi o Whakatu gratefully acknowledges the contributions of the following people in the production of this book.

Project Group: Anne Rush, Judy Finn, Alison Roxburgh and Donna Hiser

Cuisine Team: Linda Walker, Nigel Petersen, Deborah Walsh, Pat Edwards, Judy Finn and Alison Roxburgh

Artistic Direction: Anne Rush, Véronique Cornille

Design: Jo Williams

Photography: Véronique Cornille, with Kevin Judd, Craig Potton, Daniel Allen, Alan Doak, Grant Stirling and Ian Trafford

Production Co-ordination: Robbie Burton, Craig Potton Publishing

Editing: Donna Hiser

Scanning: Image Centre, Auckland

Printing: Everbest Printing Co Ltd, China

First published in 2005 by The Bishop Suter Art Gallery Te Aratoi o Whakatu,
208 Bridge Street, Nelson, New Zealand.

ISBN 0-9582396-9-X

www.TheSuter.org.nz

remember, experience, dream

The Suter
Te Aratoi o Whakatu

contents

Port Puponga •   Farewell Spit

Paturau River •

                    • Collingwood

                                    Golden Bay

                • Onekaka

                                    • Separation Point
                            • Wainui Bay
                Tata Beach • • Ligar Bay
                Pohara •
                    • Takaka
        Pupu Springs •

                            Abel Tasman
                            National Park

Kahurangi National Park

                                • Sandy Bay
                                            Tasman Bay
                                • Kaiteriteri
        Riwaka River
                                • Riwaka
                                • Motueka
                Lower Moutere • • Mariri
                Motueka River
                                • Kina
                            Tasman
        Mt Arthur
                                    • Ruby Bay
                                • Atawhai
                            Mapua • • Rabbit Island
                Upper Moutere • • Mahana
                                        Nelson
                Redwood Valley •   Maitai River
                            • Appleby
                                    • Richmond
                    Brightwater   Aniseed Valley
        Tapawera •   Wakefield   Lee Valley

                                                        Marlborough Sounds

                                                                    • Blenheim

                    • Kawateri Junction

                Buller River

                            • St Arnaud
                            Lake Rotoiti
    • Murchison

        Lake Rotoroa   Mt Robert
    Nelson Lakes National Park

preface

The Outside Table is a recipe book which explores the ways in which Nelson people gather and prepare food. It looks at how a regional cuisine is evolving based on a variety of cultural influences passed from generation to generation and combined with the abundant seasonal produce available locally.

The early people of Nelson cooked and ate outside of necessity, acting out the ritual of hunting and gathering food and fuel to prepare meals in a time honoured way. Nowadays the benevolent climate encourages the practice of eating outdoors as a lifestyle choice and recreational activity. Social occasions focus around a barbecue or picnic table and areas for eating outside form an integral design feature of most Nelson homes and baches.

Just as the food of a particular region has its roots in the cultural origins of its settlers and its physical environment, so does its art. The Bishop Suter Art Gallery Te Aratoi o Whakatu has been preserving, exhibiting and celebrating the art of the Nelson region for over one hundred years and *The Outside Table* has been produced as a fundraiser to support the renovation and extension of the gallery building. A vast amount of work has been done by volunteers, with enormous support from the wider community, so that our artistic heritage can be preserved for future generations.

our sponsors

Our sincere thanks to our sponsors, without whom this book would have remained a dream.

Platinum sponsors

Cliff and Ann Nighy

Craig Potton Publishing Ltd

Fletcher Vautier Moore

McFadden McMeeken Phillips Lawyers

Nelson Pine Industries Ltd

Nimbus Advertising

The Lodge at Paratiho Farms

93More FM

Gold sponsors

Hunter Ralfe Lawyers

Irving Smith Jack Architects Ltd

Staig and Smith Ltd

Tasman Bays Food Group Ltd

The Nelson Market Ltd

Silver sponsors

Agnes and Hermann Seifried

Arthouse Architecture Ltd

Chris Hurley

Julia Carr

Nelson City Fresh Choice

Nelson Tourism Services

Neudorf Vineyards

Tresson Interior Design

Woollaston Estates

foreword

This is a book about some of the simplest joys of life. For me, it brings back wonderful childhood memories of weekly picnics with extended family and friends. They were hard times, but the Depression and the war that followed brought with them a community spirit, a togetherness and a sharing that are the source of many cherished memories. I have vivid recollections of happy times when it was a treat to be able to eat simple food, outdoors, surrounded by those we loved. The whole beautiful Nelson and Tasman region was our dining room and our 'outside table' was usually a rug on the ground.

Our picnics took us to many places – geographically as well as gastronomically. Perhaps a trout baked over an open fire on the banks of the Motueka River; a roasted chicken at the source of the Riwaka; home-cured ham with eggs at Pupu Springs; sandwiches, peaches and cream at Lake Rotoiti; or cockles boiled in a billy at Sandy Bay. Even today, I prefer a grilled sausage wrapped in lavishly buttered bread to a meal at the Ritz or the Savoy! Wherever we went, whatever we ate, one thing never changed – my grandfather collected the kindling, lit the fire and boiled the billy. Billy tea was the order of the day. Perhaps that is why I now seem to favour woody Chardonnay.

My personal passions, and I'm sure I'm not alone in this, are included in the pages ahead – this beautiful Nelson/Tasman region that offers so much variety in the landscape; our dynamic people and their histories; our wonderful New Zealand art; and the fine food and wine that comes from the land and the sea. My wife Hilary and I feel a deep connection to this region. Her family, the Duncans, arrived in Nelson from Scotland in 1842 on board the *Fifeshire*. My great great grandfather Thomas Goodman, an apprentice baker from Nottingham in England, arrived here in 1843. Seven generations on, the Goodman family still have interests in the food industry.

Another part of this region's history is The Bishop Suter Art Gallery, which has been a cultural hub for over a century now. In the same way as The Suter cherishes their significant permanent collection of New Zealand art, we need to cherish The Suter, and treat it like the treasure it is. That means allowing it to grow and serve the next generations by being relevant and inspiring. The Suter Project aims to provide that new facility, and the funds from the sale of *The Outside Table* will help ensure the art legacy we leave for the future.

I am immensely proud of this delightful book, and I'd like to congratulate the team of Suter supporters who worked so hard on it, volunteering their skills. I hope it spends time in your kitchen as well as on the coffee table, and encourages families to gather together more often to enjoy the simple pleasures of good food, companionship and the ever-changing landscape.

Sir Patrick Goodman

PCNZM, Kt.Bach., CBE

Patron of The Bishop Suter Art Gallery Te Aratoi o Whakatu

introduction

It may be a vine-covered courtyard to the rear of a Victorian villa, or a bungalow garden enclosed by trees. It could be a veranda with views of Tasman Bay, or merely a suburban deck with a gas barbecue. Regardless of how we picture the sunny Nelson idyll, there is one constant element - the outside table. Everything, after all, tastes better outdoors, with fresh air, scented plants and birdsong to stimulate the appetite. In every culture, paradise is depicted as a garden, and the allure of dining *al fresco*, in weather so balmy it is pleasant to sit outside even after sunset, has surely been an influence in the recent population influx to the Nelson region.

To northern Europeans, it is a familiar scenario; even before Elizabeth David enthralled a post-war generation with her story of 'sea and sun and olive trees', the English upper classes had swarmed to the warm south and all but colonised the French Riviera. Modern Nelson, like the south of France and the Mediterranean region generally, offers fresh ingredients grown in a climate that both differentiates and defines them: the freshest fish, intensely flavoured vine-ripened tomatoes, red peppers, glistening eggplants, basil grown in sunshine, the first cold pressings of green olive oil – all elements of a diet now thought to be the healthiest in the world.

Closely associated with Nelson's benign climate has been a range of alternative lifestyles, attracting those with artistic or horticultural ambitions which do not confine them to living in a big city. These range from artists like Colin McCahon, Doris Lusk and Rita Angus in the 1930s and 1940s to people like Wolfgang Mann who has sold organic produce at the Nelson market for sixteen years. From the pacifist orchardists who congregated in the Moutere and in the Riverside Community after the war, the English potters of the 1960s, to all manner of religious sects and tiny schismatic churches, Nelson has played host to non-conformists, artists and bohemians one and all, many of them from continental Europe. With this cosmopolitan influx has come a more open attitude to food, reflected in the wide range of vegetables and fruit to be found on sale at the Nelson market. This influence can be seen in our outside fare, too. My own family has long enjoyed a version of spanakopita, adapted to local conditions, using silver beet instead of spinach, and cheddar taking the place of feta. We Nelsonians have also adopted a relaxed attitude to table manners. Nowadays it is okay to use your fingers on a picnic, but our Victorian ancestors would have been shocked; plates, knives, forks, spoons, table cloth and serviettes were all on Mrs Beeton's list of essential items for a picnic luncheon for twenty.

The earliest Nelson settlers were certainly familiar with the outside table: houses were small and kitchens hot so, whenever the weather permitted, meals were eaten outside. But, regardless of the weather, all cooking had to be done outside over an open fire, perhaps with a rough fireplace or makeshift shelter over it. On rainy days, those with an umbrella might be able to hold it up with one hand while they stirred with the other, but Sarah Greenwood of Motueka, for one, complained in a letter to her mother in 1843, 'In the course of the day I got wet almost to the waist by cooking out of doors.'

For the first Nelson settlers vegetable and fruit gardens were not so much a romance as a necessity, and an account of horticultural prizes in a forerunner of the A & P Show reported in the *Nelson Examiner* of 1847 reveals a surprising diversity of produce: potatoes, turnips, onions, cabbage, carrots, parsnips, pumpkins, apples, peaches, rhubarb and plums might all be expected, but prizes were also awarded for horseradish, broad beans, kidney beans and alpine strawberries. Perhaps the most interesting was a prize for tomatoes, which became popular in Nelson only from the 1920s, when Italian immigrants established glasshouses in The Wood. Men traditionally took on responsibility for growing vegetables, whilst women tended the flowerbeds and did the housework. Most households also bought produce from greengrocers however, especially as increasing urbanisation resulted in smaller sections with less scope for a vegetable patch. In the mid twentieth century market gardens were established at Hope to meet the increasing demand for store-bought vegetables.

Today, seafood is a highlight of Nelson's outside table, but this too is a modern construct, borrowed from the Mediterranean. It is no wonder the Nelson fishing industry was slow to get established, for quite apart from the problem of keeping fish fresh, the early fishing industry had to fight deeply entrenched prejudice. In England, fish had been the despised food of the poor, whilst red meat had been the preserve of the middle class and the rich. For immigrants, arriving in a country where beef and lamb could – and was – eaten three times a day, this soon became a matter of great pride, often mentioned in letters home. Fish could have no place in this working class Utopia.

Even beach life as we now know it did not exist for the Victorians, who were extremely circumspect about exposing their bare skin – umbrella shaped hats and ankle-length dresses saw to that. A beach was not for swimming – at least, not for mixed groups of male and female swimmers. During whatever 'bathing' took place, men and women were strictly segregated (though curiously, such arrangements presented the opportunity to swim naked, particularly amongst the men). Then there was the horse-drawn bathing shed on wheels, which was backed out into the surf far enough for the swimmer to make a modest two second appearance from the back door and step down directly into the water. More often, people remained in their formal street clothes, and simply paddled near the waterline in bare feet. The sea was regarded as dangerous, and reported shark sightings out in Tasman Bay were enough to scare people off completely.

Beach culture as we now know it began only in the 1920s, culminating in the mid 20th century. How radically different from the limited Victorian experiences were my constant childhood and teenage visits to Tahunanui beach, surfing the rare good waves, but mostly lounging on a beach towel without a thought to sunburn. Our annual holidays were spent at Stephens Bay near Kaiteriteri, where there would be a great deal more lying about on the beach with my siblings and relations. Tucked behind a rocky lookout on the pinnacle of the hill overlooking the bay was the holiday bach to which we had regular access - Uncle Tom's Cabin. The name was professionally sign-written on a board to one side of the veranda – the one part of the bach which was properly constructed in wood. Built during the 1930s Depression, its walls (like many other Kiwi baches) had been clad with flattened kerosene tins. Cooking was done in a tiny Atlas oven; there was no refrigerator, only a safe and, needless to say, the toilet was a long drop out the back. Often our outside table was the veranda, where we would eat our lunch of lettuce salad with tomatoes, tinned beetroot and Highlander condensed milk 'mayonnaise', and gorge on the yellow plums from the tree overhanging the bach. Somehow they always seemed to be ripe during our holidays there.

Down a steep track to the rear of the bach was a cove called Tapu. It never occurred to us that the name might have been conferred for some reason, as we merrily gathered pipis from the abundant shoals and took them back to the bach to steam them open. Perhaps the inevitable grit deterred the adults, for they rarely joined us in the feast. Such was not the case for the Washbourn family of Golden Bay. In *Courage and Camp Ovens*, Inga Washbourn recalls digging for pipis, cockles and tuatuas, and pulling mussels off the rocks, 'Mussel and pipi stews were always popular made with onion, parsley and thyme in a white sauce – a favourite family dish to this day.'

Similarly, an old-timer recalled (to Christine Hunt for her book *Speaking a Silence*) that the Collingwood community would gather informally for Sunday picnics during the interwar years, when communal kerosene tins of mussels would be boiled on the beach. All the families needed to take along was a basket of bread and butter. However, the taste for mussels was not necessarily universal among the early English settlers. Inga Washbourn quotes (also in *Speaking a Silence*) a newly arrived clergyman talking to her Victorian ancestor, Elizabeth:

'Mussels', said he, 'why, you don't eat those?'

'Yes, certainly, and very good they are.'

'Ah!' said he shudderingly, 'A Maori woman gave me one.'

'Was it cooked?'

'Oh no, I ate it *au naturel* with the utmost horror - don't remind me of it.'

At which, Elizabeth assures us, she had a good laugh.

More familiar to English tastes were the flounder which local Maori taught the early settlers of Collingwood to spear at night in shallow water, using flax torches to attract them. In return, 19th century Maori were introduced to the delights of Pakeha outdoor cooking in the form of rice pudding. The Washbourns would hold Bible readings on Sundays on their front lawn, attended by Maori who would come from the pas (Maori villages) then situated at Tukurua and Puramahoi. Afterwards, a fire would be lit beneath a large outside boiler, and rice and sugar would be tipped in and stirred with fresh milk from the family farm. Silence would then reign as the Maori visitors scooped up every last morsel, using empty mussel shells as spoons.

As the Victorian age progressed, picnics became ever more elaborate, with cakes, pies, sausage rolls and platters of sandwiches. There was the growing institution of the garden party, with its then implied informality, such as that held for the Governor, Lord Onslow, on his visit to Nelson in 1886. What amounted to an open invitation was published beforehand in the *Nelson Evening Mail*, which led to much speculation among readers as to who could be considered sufficiently a part of Nelson 'society' to attend. Few would have felt this more acutely than Emily Harris, a woman of privileged birth then living in much reduced circumstances. Nevertheless, she donned the one good dress the family owned and went along, discovering to her relief that most of her friends were there, later noting in her diary that the difference between New Zealand and Britain for a person of her small income was that back home she would have had only two or three families to call upon, whereas in Nelson she had fifty.

The same egalitarian sense of free-for-all reigned at the sports meetings which attracted huge public interest in rural areas. The Tadmor Sports Meeting of November 9, 1906 included running, jumping, and wood chopping. For the children, there were lolly scrambles (with boiled lollies only – no wrapped sweets back then), sack races, three-legged races and the egg and spoon. Everyone brought a picnic lunch and the atmosphere can't have been too different from the Sunday school picnics on the Maitai River I remember as a child some 50 years later.

Our family picnics in the Lee and Aniseed Valleys often lasted the entire day and into the early part of the evening. My mother would pack a wicker picnic hamper with sandwiches, often a bacon and egg pie, the makings of a salad, fruit and a tin of home baking: ginger crunch, chocolate chippies, perhaps a sultana fruit cake. Sometimes we sizzled sausages held on a long wire fork over the embers of a fire. The feast would be set out on a huge triangular piece of camouflage-patterned canvas brought back from the war in Egypt by my father.

The North African campaign also gave rise to the Benghazi burner, later to become an icon of the post-war New Zealand picnic. Better known under its trade name of the *Thermette*, this contraption is still being manufactured, though few of the younger generation would be familiar with its workings: a fire of twigs in the centre of the *Thermette* heats the jacket of water which surrounds it, producing boiling water within minutes. Previously water had been boiled in a billy to make tea, whether at a picnic or at the morning and afternoon teas ('tea-o') served to the seasonal workers on Nelson's orchards, hop and berry farms. It was often the job of the farmer's children to take the ready-made billies of tea across the fields to the workers, although outdoor labourers in more remote areas were not always as lucky; for them, it was a matter of leaving the house in the morning with an old gin bottle filled with lukewarm tea.

The billy went hand in hand with another essential piece of outside cooking equipment – the camp oven. These heavy cast iron pots always had a tight fitting lid and a handle to allow suspension over an open fire. A family or a logging crew at a bush camp usually possessed two camp ovens – one for pot-roasting meat, and a large round one for baking bread and scones. Yeast starters had to be brewed from hops and potatoes, and often the kneaded dough would be placed, in the camp oven, next to a roaring fire to prove. When the fire had died down somewhat, the oven was placed directly over the embers with more live embers piled on top to ensure even baking.

Camp ovens are rare now, but they were still in use by Golden Bay gold miners as late as the 1930s. The miners often camped in bivouacs of ponga logs covered over with a fly and did all of their cooking outdoors. Sea-pie was commonly on the menu, as was baked meat and plum duff. To eke out the meat, there were flour and butter dumplings known as *doughboys* or, less delicately, as *buggers afloat*. Currants and raisins were added to make a dessert version, to be eaten with sweetened condensed milk. Nikau palm hearts were eaten raw, boiled and pickled, and there were generally eels in the creeks to be caught. Occasionally the miners would find a wild bee hive in a dead tree and a little dynamite would be used to blast the bees to smithereens before scooping out the honey-laden wax.

Early settlers living near the coast gathered seaweed from the rocks, blanched it and turned it into a jelly by soaking it in milk with a little sugar and vanilla. In areas where the land had been cleared by burning, wild cape gooseberries would soon appear, while around the steep coastal cliffs of both Nelson and Golden Bay were vast areas of wild banana passionfruit, which still exist today. But the outside larder's most important provision was freshly caught game. The settlers had been taught by local Maori how to snare kaka and often a kaka was kept as a pet to attract other birds with his call. Kaka were also shot with the early muzzle loading rifles and eaten, as were kereru or wood pigeons. Kiwi were hunted with dogs and the explorer Skeet, making his way through the mountains between the Takaka and Buller rivers in 1861, found that with two dogs he could catch fifteen or twenty kiwi in an evening – enough to provide a staple item of diet for his men. The kiwi were said to taste a little like pork. When these birds had been hunted to the brink of extinction, the settlers turned to wild deer and 'Captain Cooker' pigs for sustenance.

Nelson's first red deer were turned out into the wild in 1861 and by the 1930s deer hunting had become a profitable business as well as a sport. In *Footprints*, an account of the early settlement of Nelson's back country, J N W Newport recalls that pigs were plentiful in most localities before white settlers arrived. In the Wangapeka Valley they existed in their thousands and pig hunting provided a major source of recreation for the young men of the Nelson back districts, as indeed it does to this day.

I no longer live in Nelson, but I visit regularly and am nearly always able to bring together family and friends with a picnic of some sort. To sit around a camp fire with a pan of venison back steaks sizzling over the embers, or to steam a billy full of sweet blue-lipped mussels at the beach, is to connect with both our contemporaries and our ancestors in the most convivial way we know - through the outside table.

This book is a Nelson work – stories and recipes brought together by people who love the region and who are raising funds to support The Suter Gallery, Nelson's regional art museum. *The Outside Table* contains a taste of many of the good things of Nelson – good food, good wine, the company of friends and a breath of fresh air.

David Burton

David Burton is New Zealand's most awarded food writer and is the author of six books including *200 Years of New Zealand Food & Cookery*. He is a restaurant critic and contributes regularly on food and drink matters to *Cuisine*, *The Dominion Post* and *The Press*.

beach cook-up
at wainui bay

In summer the ultimate Kiwi dream is to head to the bach for a holiday at the beach and to catch and eat local seafood to your heart's content. In Nelson, with its balmy climate, beautiful beaches and abundance of seafood, that dream is a summer ritual.

Wainui Bay on the northwestern edge of the Abel Tasman National Park in Golden Bay has been a source of kai moana, ever since the Maori discovered its rich coastal resources hundreds of years ago. Traces of middens used by Maori have been found on numerous sites along the Golden Bay coastline, stretching from Separation Point in the east to Farewell Spit in the west. Wide expanses of golden sand sheltered by sculptured granite headlands are fed by the nutrient-rich Wainui River. The low tide channels, with etched tidal patterns and bars, are a natural habitat for a wide range of coastal dwellers and locals can often be observed gathering mussels, rock oysters, scallops, crabs, cockles and pipis or setting their nets for whitebait, flounder, snapper and other fishy species.

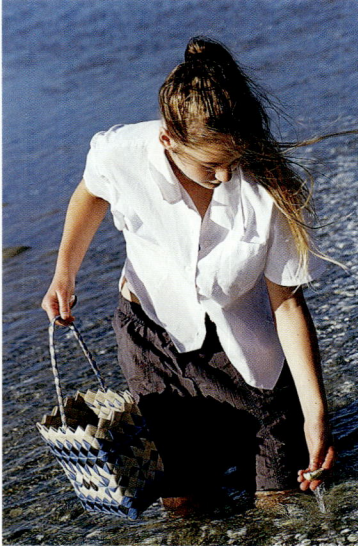

At Wainui Bay a commercial mussel farm can be observed as you drive over the hill from Pohara, Tata Beach and Ligar Bay; the lines of black floats create a grid pattern that is easily recognisable. This proximity promotes the spawning of green-lipped mussels (*Perna canaliculus*) on the adjoining rocky headlands below the high water line. Mussels are plentiful in the region, and along with scallops reap major export returns. The less adventurous holiday maker, who finds scrambling over rocks at low tide daunting, can pick up live mussels from tanks at local supermarkets and fish shops. Mussels are a versatile shellfish and can be poached whole in wine or beer and eaten with crusty bread, or steamed and chopped for beach fritters and chowders. Like mussels, rock oysters cling to the rocks below the high tide mark in distinctive colonies. They are challenging little critters to harvest, and are best eaten as soon as they are prised from their rock with the help of a trusty pocket knife. Raw oysters are an acquired taste, but devotees wax lyrical of their virtue and flavour and they need little by way of accompaniment.

Scallops are declared by many to be the ultimate holiday catch. A boat and a scallop dredge are required to harvest these delectable shellfish from the sea bed in the shallow waters of Tasman and Golden Bays and for recreational fisherman there are strict regulations regarding time of harvest, size and numbers permitted per person. Once the shell has been opened and the 'skirt' removed they are wonderful toasted briefly in the half shells on a grill over the fire.

Whitebait (the very young fish of various *Galaxias* species) have been a Kiwi favourite for generations, and local restaurants serve traditional whitebait fritters and chips with salad whenever 'the bait are running' (in Golden Bay the season starts on 15 August and ends on the last day of November). These tiny fish travel in shoals up river from the sea to spawn and, in the season, all major rivers and streams in the Bay host whitebaiters, who wait patiently with their nets on the incoming tide.

Paddle crabs (*Ovalipes catharus*) are plentiful in Golden Bay and can be harvested in a variety of ways - but all require commitment. The simplest way is to bait crab pots with fish heads and weight them to the sandy ocean floor just below the low tide mark, returning to check the pots on the subsequent low tide. A more hair-raising method is to wade into the tide wearing a snorkel and mask - with feet well protected too! Once a crab is sighted pluck the creature's back shell nimbly between your thumb and forefinger in such a way to avoid the crab's pincers. They can nip most painfully if you miss! A trusty assistant is required to hold a bucket in which to toss the crabs and to provide ample praise and encouragement. Family and friends are essential to orchestrate shrieks and *encores* from the shore when the hunter scores a strike.

Paddle crab is best cooked and served straight from the sea. Bring a generous sized pot of salted water to the boil, add the crab and bring the water back to boiling point. Boil for another seven minutes before plunging the crab into a bucket of cold sea water. Next place the crab on a board with its belly up and cut into pieces using a sterilised pair of garden secateurs to cut through the body, legs and claws. Pick out delicious white crab meat with toothpicks or small metal skewers while you socialise. Once cooked, crabmeat will keep in the fridge for a couple of days, and is delicious for crab cakes or salads.

At Wainui Bay cockles embedded in the tidal flats are a culinary favourite as well as being easy to gather for less adventurous diners. Preparing a feast here, on the beach, differs markedly from contemporary gas barbecue cooking. It is about appreciating the simple pleasures of life and about returning to the rituals of our forebears. The flavours are rich and full, and need little embellishment, and the extended exploration to find the cockle beds and the sea lettuce will hone your appetite and reveal the hunter-gatherer within.

Prior planning is essential, and you may want to make a reconnaissance trip to choose a location and to collect firewood from above the high tide line. It pays to check out the strict regulations relating to harvesting fish and shellfish and restrictions on gathering times that apply. You are likely to need a fire permit too. Local regulations are usually found on public signage at beaches and boat ramps and if in doubt the local Department of Conservation offices have a wealth of knowledge to share.

Gather and socialise when the tide is lowest so that family and friends can fill large sacks with dry driftwood before harvesting the shellfish beds for succulent cockles. Keep an eye out for emerald green sea lettuce, or parengo, for the potato dumplings, remembering to take only what you intend to eat. Parengo is quite unmistakable as a bright green seaweed which looks like limp lettuce or cabbage leaves floating in shallow water. Best harvested in sheltered areas, it needs to be well rinsed to rid it of sand and grit and then drained and tossed very lightly in a pan with garlic oil or butter to bring out its subtle sea-like flavour.

The setting up of the feasting camp, the construction of a good fire pit, the food gathering, preparation and final cooking all take time. But it is time which reminds us of what is of value, allows us to be absorbed by the character of a special place and allows us to see the changing light on sand, sea and mountain backdrop. The exercise, fresh air, and sand between the toes will also help to develop a hearty appetite and the culinary results will easily justify your exertions. Your firepit needs to be no more than a metre in diameter and half a metre deep, and is easily dug in sand. The base and sides of the pit should be lined with large rocks that will act as a hearth on which to build the fire and will retain the heat to cook the food.

Fill the pit with driftwood of various sizes and establish a vigorous fire. When the wood has burned away and a deep base of embers remains, the stones will have reached a high enough temperature to cook the food. Rake across the embers and make the bottom of the pit as level as possible. Put the harvested cockles (still in their shells) into a wet jute sack and place the sack into the fire pit on top of the embers. Cover the sack with a layer of seaweed to assist steaming, and then shovel damp sand on top of the sack, rocks and embers to seal the oven. Let the cockles steam in their own juices for about an hour before unearthing them and tipping them onto a large platter. Pour the coconut cream dressing over the cockles and eat on the beach in the company of friends and family. When the evening conversations and feasting are over the fire pit is easily filled leaving no trace that you were ever there.

Linda Walker

tata beach lentil soup with cockles

This soup is easily made entirely on the beach on a charcoal burner or over the open fire.

1 tablespoon olive oil
1 medium onion, diced
2 cloves garlic
1 teaspoon fresh ginger, peeled and grated
½ teaspoon tumeric
1 fresh red chilli, finely diced (or prepared red curry paste to taste)

1 cup red lentils
2 cups water
1 400ml can coconut cream
lemon juice to taste
about 300g cockle meat
salt to taste
shredded sea lettuce, parsley or coriander

Heat the oil in a pot or billy.

Fry onion in the oil until golden brown, stir in garlic and ginger and add turmeric and chilli to taste (or omit these spices and use prepared red curry paste).

Fry for a few seconds more.

Add lentils and fry, stirring, for about two minutes.

Add two cups of water and bring to the boil, stirring occasionally.

Add 1½ cups of extra water or a can of coconut cream and cook for another 20 minutes or until the lentils are soft.

Add the juice of a lemon and the cockles and check for seasoning.

To serve, garnish with shredded sea lettuce, parsley or coriander.

coconut cream dressing for cockles

To save on precious holiday time jars of seasoned coconut cream and spiced oil can be prepared in advance at home.

2 ripe red chillies (or a splash of bottled sweet chilli sauce if you are a nervous chilli eater)
1 clove garlic
1 tablespoon sugar (if not using sweet chilli sauce)

1 lime (or lemon)
1 tablespoon vinegar
4 tablespoons fish sauce
1 400ml can coconut cream
1 bunch of coriander or parsley

Cut chillies down the centre, remove seeds, and pound in a mortar and pestle with the garlic (or chop finely).

Mix in the sugar and the juice and pulp of the lime.

Stir in the vinegar, fish sauce and coconut cream and add the coarsely chopped greens. Spoon over the cockles.

These flavours are also excellent added to the beach lentil soup.

beach damper

Making damper is a favourite holiday activity, and can keep children entertained for a long time observing the 'folly' of cooking in the old ways.

3 cups flour   25g butter
3 teaspoons baking powder   approximately 1 cup milk
pinch of salt

Mix the flour, baking powder and salt, and rub in the butter.

Mix in enough milk to form a soft dough.

Choose driftwood sticks that are long enough to spike into the sand near the embers of the fire pit or long enough to safely hold over the fire.

Wrap a piece of the scone dough around a driftwood stick so that only one end of the stick pokes out.

Cook over the fire until golden brown.

Take the damper off the stick and fill the hole with butter and runny bush honey, or anything else that takes your fancy!

planked fish

Fillets of fish rubbed with garlic and lemon can be roasted in a fire pit on a plank of wood retrieved from the high water mark. Whole Anatoki organic salmon have been cooked at Tata Beach in this way.

Lash a whole fish or firm fish fillets to a drift wood plank with plaited harakeke (flax) as shown in the photograph. The fire needs to be lit some time in advance so as to allow a reasonable depth of hot embers to build up with little naked flame. When the fire is at this stage position the end of the plank well into the sand at an angle where the whole fish or fillets face downwards towards the fire which should be hot enough to seal in the juices and sear the fish.

Let the embers burn low to cook the fish all the way through and develop a smoky flavour. The length of the cooking time will depend on the size of your fish, but the fish will be cooked when it has turned white throughout. Allow a longer roasting time for whole roasted fish; not so long for fish filets.

The result is succulent and moist.

scallops on the beach

To prepare the scallops remove the top shell with a sharp knife, lift out the scallops and clean them. Place them back in the half shell and baste each with a small knob of salted butter or a half teaspoon of olive oil.

Place the shells on a heated charcoal burner or in a cast iron pan over the open fire
Cook over a medium heat for about two minutes until just cooked through.
Shellfish cook very quickly and will toughen if overcooked.
Dust with a little Grassmere flaky sea salt and eat immediately.

kiwi whitebait tart

Whitebaiting is a favourite seasonal occupation, particularly in the rivers and estuaries near Collingwood in Golden Bay and at Paturau on the west coast of Golden Bay.

If you are lucky enough to net some whitebait for a beach picnic you will no doubt want to cook them in the time honoured way of dredging them with flour, tossing them in a pan with hot butter and serving with black pepper and a squeeze of lemon. However, this recipe is a useful variation in the use of whitebait when it is in plentiful supply. It makes a tart 25cm in diameter.

Pastry

125g cold butter
2 cups flour, white or wholemeal
pinch of salt

1 teaspoon baking powder
cold water to mix

Grate the butter into the flour and add the salt and baking powder. Mix together with just enough cold water to bind.
Roll out the pastry and line a 25cm tart plate. A sprinkle of semolina or polenta on the tin before you line it will assist at removal time.
Chill the pastry while you make the filling.

Filling

3 eggs
¼ cup milk
¼ cup cream
2 teaspoons dill leaves, chopped

½ teaspoon each of white pepper
and salt
grated zest of one lemon
500g whitebait

Beat together the eggs, milk, cream, dill, pepper, salt and lemon zest, then stir in the whitebait.
Pour the mixture into the prepared shell.
Bake for approximately 45 minutes at 180°C.

potato dumplings cooked in seawater served with sea lettuce and garlic butter

These dumplings should not be made too far in advance as they will become sticky and difficult to handle. However, you can cook the potato in advance (or use left over mashed potato) and the dish will proceed very quickly.

sea lettuce	1 medium egg, beaten
garlic butter	2 cups flour
2½ cups cold mashed potato	½ teaspoon salt

Have friends or the children collect sea lettuce at low tide and soak in a bucket of fresh water. Just before dinner give it a good wash and drain it well.

Garlic butter can be purchased, or make your own allowing for your own preference of garlic intensity.

Cook the potatoes in boiling salted water until tender. Drain them, return to the pan and mash, allowing as much water as possible to evaporate. Don't puree the potatoes in a blender or food processor as they will become gluey.

When the potatoes have cooled, mix in the egg. Then, reserving two tablespoons of the flour, mix most of the remaining flour into the potato and egg with the salt. The amount of flour needed depends partly on the type of potatoes used. You want a dough that is quite soft but firm enough to handle. Knead the dough very lightly.

Break off pieces of the dough and roll into little sausages as thick as your thumb. Cut them up into 2.5cm lengths and dust lightly with the remaining flour. Once made keep the dumplings cool, in a single layer, on a floured plate until it is time to cook them.

To cook, bring a billy of sea water to a simmer over a fire (or a large pot of salted water to a simmer on your stove). Tip the dumplings carefully into the water.

They take almost no time to cook; as soon as they float they should be lifted out with a slotted spoon. Put them straight into a pan with sizzling garlic butter, swirling them around a little so as to coat the dumplings on all sides. Add the well-drained sea lettuce, swirl again, and spoon onto a heated serving dish.

watercress dressed with spiced olive oil

Gather your own watercress if you have access to a clean stream or purchase it from your local market.

1 teaspoon fennel seeds	½ teaspoon salt
1 tablespoon cumin seeds	1 cup olive oil
2 cloves garlic	watercress

Warm the fennel and cumin seeds in a small pan until they smell fragrant.
Remove from the heat.
Finely chop the garlic with the salt.
Stir the seeds and garlic into the olive oil and pour into a screw top jar.
Store in a chilli bin or fridge and use within a few days.
Dress the watercress just before serving.

a magical celebration

'Adults are obsolete children.' (Dr Seuss)

Often our most vivid childhood memories are of parties - flashes of fairy bread and cheerios; party dresses and pirate costumes; jelly and balloons.

The best parties begin decorously, children gathered around a treasure-laden table, and end uproariously, covered in crumbs and cream, party hats askew and clutching prizes from pass-the-parcel and musical chairs. And then there are the cakes! Jolly trains, teddy bears and rugby balls lovingly created in Kiwi kitchens by mums of varying abilities. There are tidy cakes carefully copied from women's magazines and baroque lolly-encrusted masterpieces by the more wildly creative mums. There are the classics; kiwifruit garnished pavlovas and sticky banana cakes, and the newcomers: towering choux pastry croquembouches and Mississippi mud cakes. Let's not forget the savouries; those old favourites, saveloys (or little boys – with their faithful sidekick, tomato sauce), tiny sausage rolls, prickly toothpick hedgehogs of cheese and pineapple, asparagus rolls and more.

As delightful as the party table may be, there are other equally important rituals to consider. First the greeting of guests and accepting of gifts must be accomplished. With younger children, this can be a particularly chaotic time as parents attempt to disentangle themselves from shy children in party frocks and the birthday child rips paper and discards presents with wild abandon. Once this has been achieved and the children have been successfully ushered to the table and seated, the party can begin. The demolition of the party table is done in short order and the children, fortified with goodies, can begin the timeless work of birthdays – the party games.

As de Montaigne said, 'Children's plays are not sports and should be deemed as their most serious actions'. Who can forget the primal terrors of their first game of hide and seek? Holding one's breath, heart thumping as footsteps approach, shrieking upon being discovered. Pass the parcel and musical chairs are other perennial favourites. With each disappearing chair or paper wrapping the excitement grows, the wait for the music to stop becomes interminable and, ultimately, there is the prize for the lucky child. Outside, an adult with a whistle can be an advantage as statues, obstacle courses, treasure hunts, and 'what's the time Mr. Wolf' all benefit from a little marshalling and good timekeeping.

There are many great sites in the Nelson region for a children's party. Rabbit Island is a local favourite. A long pine plantation with a beach on one side and wetlands on the other, it is popular with 'kids' of all ages for its excellent swimming, wonderful sandy beach and towering pine trees. There is room for everyone to spread out with many large grassed picnic areas dotted among the trees. Kaiteriteri beach and its neighbouring bays, with golden sands and interesting rocky outcrops, also provide many perfect locations for memorable children's parties. Close to Nelson and boasting a zoo, hydro slide, mini-golf, tennis and well-stocked playgrounds, Tahunanui beach is a perennial favourite with local kids and visitors alike. In the scorching heat of a Nelson summer, a day up river is a tempting option. There are many lovely swimming holes in the Maitai Valley, only minutes from the city, or the more adventurous can pack a picnic and inner tubes and head out to the Wairoa Gorge.

Textile artist Sue Bevin chose the delightfully surreal Jester House on the Tasman Highway for her daughter Ella's fourth birthday party. Sue's career began early; at three years of age she was already cutting up curtains and bedspreads for her creations. She has been sewing for as long as she can remember, inspired by her mother who made clothes for the people of the Ministry of Works villages in which her family lived. These days she continues the theme, creating gorgeous one-off garments from her collection of vintage fabrics. Her busy hands have ensured that Ella and her friends have delightful party frocks for the occasion.

Jester House is a friendly, fun and family-oriented café between Nelson and Motueka. Established in 1991 by Steve and Jude Richards, it quickly gained a reputation as the place for both kids and adults to have a great time. Jude and Steve's whimsical style of fun and art is embodied in their wondrous garden. At Jester House you can feed tame eels – or 'charismatic megafauna' as Steve likes to call them. You can get lost in the maze or play a game on the giant's chessboard. A wander through the rambling garden reveals quirky artworks and delightful Alice-in-Wonderland touches.

The Boot guest cottage is a fairytale come to life. Designed by the Richards as a luxurious retreat from the everyday world, it is also the perfect backdrop for Ella's magic cupcake castle. Artist and cook Nigel Peterson whipped up this cardboard castle complete with drawbridge, ivy and turrets. The more turrets the better as this is an interactive cake! To make one yourself you will need some cardboard boxes, tubes of paint, a glue gun and an active imagination. Construct the basic castle shape first and then glue on painted cardboard squares to imitate stonework. Add cardboard turrets, a portcullis, drawbridge, ivy and pennants for a truly splendid castle. Provide bowls of brightly coloured icing for the children to dip their cupcakes into and sprinkles to top their cakes. Once the children have dipped and decorated their cakes, they place them on the castle.

This is the perfect moment for a rousing chorus of 'Happy Birthday to You' before the magic cupcake castle is chaotically deconstructed.

The party table holds a cornucopia of delights: wiggly woggly sandwiches and eel-shaped grissini pay homage to the slimy characters that lurk under the Jester's bridge. There are toffee apples on sticks, a liquorice tui, jellies, sweetheart cookies, creamy fudge, feijoa and honey slushy and more. Naturally, no Jester House picnic would be complete without the famous jesterbread men biscuits. These were hidden around the garden and Steve obligingly led the children on a treasure hunt to discover them. After another round of party games, another glass of Moutere apple water and just one more outrageous cupcake, the party drew to a close.

As with the greeting of guests, dispersing them can be a trifle tricky and timing is everything. Too soon and the children will be disappointed, too long after the combination of party food and adrenalin has worn off and disastrous scenes can result. Get it right and the kids will leave contentedly, looking forward to the next magical birthday bash.

'The child is a curly, dimpled lunatic.' (Ralph Waldo Emerson)

Deborah Walsh

grissini eels

These wriggly critters will delight the children and make a great 'dipper' for adult fare too.

300ml warm water
1 teaspoon dried yeast
500g unbleached bakers' flour

2 teaspoons salt
semolina - for scattering on baking trays

Place water in the bowl of an electric mixer fitted with a dough hook.

Stir in the yeast, leave for a few minutes to dissolve, then add the flour and salt.

Beat well for at least five minutes (10 minutes if you are doing it by hand).

Cover the bowl and leave in a warm place to rise for 1-2 hours.

After the first rise, gently ease the dough out of the bowl and onto a workbench or marble slab.

Fold the dough into four, return it to the bowl, and leave in a warm place again to rise for 1½ hours.

Heat the oven to 200°C and sprinkle baking trays with fine semolina.

Remove the dough from the bowl gently and divide into 30g or walnut size pieces.

With your hands roll each piece of dough into a long thin shape and place onto the prepared trays, giving each piece a few twists and turns to create an eel shape.

If you have some kitchen snips at hand you can cut a mouth at one end of each eel. To create a scaly finish on the back use the kitchen snips and repeatedly make shallow nicks down the length of the breadstick.

Alternatively black sesame seeds may be scattered down the length of each bread eel.

Cook eels for about 15 minutes until golden and crunchy.

If you wish to store them for future use, reduce the temperature and oven dry them for a little longer.

Serve with savoury dips.

moutere apple water

This simple but refreshing drink takes advantage of the abundance of delicious apples in the Nelson district.

8 cooking apples, quartered
½ cup sugar
1 litre boiling water

lemon slices
applemint leaves

Place the apples in an ovenproof dish and sprinkle with the sugar.

Bake at 180°C for 30 minutes, or until soft.

Mash fruit, add boiling water, and steep until cool.

Strain through muslin and chill.

Serve garnished with lemon slices and applemint leaves.

wiggly woggly sandwiches

Try making these sandwiches with colourful fillings to make them even more interesting to small guests.

1 loaf of bread sliced lengthways - many bakeries offer this service
a tasty filling or two, eg cream cheese mixed with finely diced sun-dried tomatoes, Marmite and lettuce, peanut butter and alfalfa sprouts
kebab skewers

Make the sandwiches in the usual way with the chosen filling.
Cut the crusts from the sandwiches, slice each into 25mm strips, and weave onto the skewers creating undulating wiggly-woggly sandwiches.

feijoa and honey slushy

Many home gardens in Nelson boast a couple of feijoa trees and each tree can produce enough fruit to satisfy a whole neighbourhood! The feijoas need to be ripe and sweet for this delicious slushy, which is a great way to use up surplus fruit.

400g feijoas, peeled   3½ tablespoons sugar
100g honey   100ml water

Puree the feijoas in a blender or food processor. Combine the honey, sugar and water in a saucepan and bring slowly to the boil, stirring slowly to dissolve the sugar.
Mix the pureed feijoas into the sugar syrup and leave to cool.
Pour into a large freezer-proof bowl, cover and freeze until almost set. For a smooth texture transfer the mixture to a food processor and whiz until broken up and well mixed. Alternatively use a fork to mash the slushy and break it up. Return the slushy to the bowl, cover and freeze again. Just before serving mash the slushy once more.

toffee apples

A wicked traditional treat, as popular as ever with young partygoers.

2 cups sugar   sweet apples
1 cup water   small sticks

Place the sugar and water in a heavy saucepan over medium heat.
Stir with a metal spoon until the sugar has dissolved, then increase the heat and bring to the boil. Do not stir once boiling point is reached.
Watch closely and boil for around 15 minutes, removing from the heat when the syrup is a light brown.
Test by dropping a little of the syrup in a bowl of cold water, where it should go crisp immediately.
Push the sticks into the calyx of the apples.
Holding the saucepan at an angle, dip each apple into the hot toffee and turn to cover completely.
Place the toffee apples onto an oiled surface until they are set.

jesterbread men

Children will love to help make these party favourites.

250g softened butter
1 cup brown sugar
1 tablespoon golden syrup
1 egg
4 cups white flour
1 teaspoon baking soda

2½ teaspoons ground ginger
1 teaspoon mixed spice
¼ teaspoon salt
pinch of white pepper
currants
glacé cherries

Cream the butter, brown sugar and golden syrup together.

Add the egg and beat well.

Sift the flour, baking soda, ginger, mixed spice, salt and pepper together and combine with the butter mixture.

Knead mixture lightly and form into a ball. Wrap in cling film and refrigerate until firm. Mixture can be frozen at this point if desired.

Remove mixture from the fridge one hour before use to soften slightly and preheat the oven to 175°C.

Roll out mixture on a floured bench to approximately four mm thick. Cut into shapes with a jester cutter (or a gingerbread man shape will suffice) and place on cool greased baking trays (or use baking paper).

Decorate with currants and cut glacé cherries. Bake 12-15 minutes until golden.

Add further decoration with icing when cool. Store in an airtight container - if they last that long!

fudge to die for

This recipe is ridiculously easy to make and really is to die for!

380g can caramel condensed milk
600g chocolate buttons or
chocolate chips

1 teaspoon vanilla essence

Put all the ingredients into a glass bowl, mix together, cover and microwave at 60% power for three minutes.

This mixture will not melt to a liquid but will form a cohesive blob (it may need a little more microwaving to ensure that the chocolate chips are entirely melted).

Blend together gently with a spatula or spoon.

Press mixture into a greased dish so that it is about three cm thick.

Chill for two hours or until fudge is firm.

Cut into small portions and toss pieces in sifted cocoa or icing sugar to keep separate.

Store in the refrigerator.

sweetheart cookies

What little girl could resist these delightful pink, heart-shaped cookies?

125g butter
75g brown sugar
1 teaspoon cinnamon
1 teaspoon mixed spice
1 teaspoon ground ginger
1 egg

125g flour
125g semolina
1 teaspoon baking powder
royal or butter cream icing
pink jelly crystals

Cream butter, sugar and spices together. Add the egg and beat well.

Mix in the dry ingredients and knead with your hands until well mixed. Roll the dough out to five mm thick and cut into heart shapes.

Bake the shapes on greased trays for about 15 minutes at 180°C.

When cool decorate the top of each biscuit with royal or butter cream icing.

Dip iced surfaces into pink jelly crystals and leave to set.

magic cupcake castle

The *pièce de résistance!* A truly wonderful – and interactive – birthday cake. Guaranteed to amuse and delight everyone whatever their age.

125g butter
100g chocolate
300g Anathoth berry jam
150g caster sugar

2 large eggs, beaten
150g self raising flour
2 cups icing sugar

Melt the butter and chocolate together in the microwave.

Add the jam, sugar and eggs and stir until well mixed.

Fold in the flour and spoon the mixture into paper cupcake cases placed in muffin tins. Fill to three-quarters full to avoid overflowing.

Bake for 15-20 minutes at 170°C.

Let the children decide how to decorate the cupcakes, and have on hand a variety of special colours and textures for this.

Icing

Stir together sifted icing sugar with a few teaspoons of hot water to reach spreading consistency.

A variety of sprinkles

Hundreds and thousands.

Coloured coconut (put desiccated coconut in a small jar with a splash of food colouring and give it a good shake).

Sugar crystals (some specialty food stores stock coloured ones).

Have the children use the cupcakes to create turrets and parapets on a castle base. For the castle in the photograph we used a hot glue gun to put together cardboard tubes and boxes and painted it with non-toxic paint.

when the boats come in

Why do we all feel so strongly about the right to go and catch a fish? Some of us probably haven't wet a line since childhood yet we all wish to preserve the opportunity to go fishing in the future, if only for the enjoyment of passing down this knowledge to our children and our grandchildren. Catching a fish off the wharf is one of those quintessential childhood experiences that most of us can relate to. The activity of fishing we can sometimes associate with a new–found sense of independence – similar to that which riding our first bike gave us. Being able to take off from home on your bike, leaving parents, chores and annoying siblings behind, to meet up with your mates and spend a lazy afternoon with feet and line dangling off a wharf somewhere – that was independence!

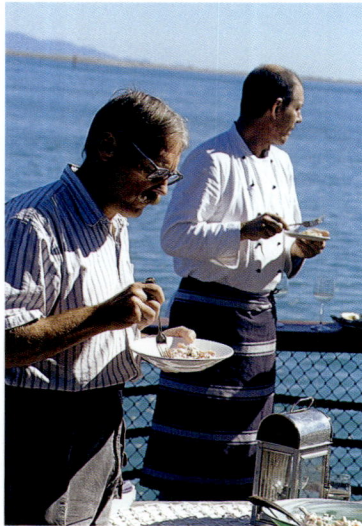

Coming home sunburnt in the early evening usually saw us learn a few more lessons, such as keeping an eye on the time, for one. I could never understand why Mum didn't regard my usual offering of a couple of leather jackets, a few spotties and the odd herring (sometimes missing a fillet or two) with more enthusiasm. Never mind, as even at this early age we were picking up a few skills in home economics such as how to look after the catch, why some species were better eating than others and the fact that meals need to be planned ahead. Thankfully the cat had no such hang-ups.

Fortunately, in this age of restricted access to commercial wharves, Port Nelson Limited has incorporated a recreational fishing space at the southern end of the main wharf, near the Wakefield Quay promenade area. Not only is this a great place to fish but it also affords marvellous views of passing traffic, from large container ships and reefers during the fruit season to small coastal vessels and the daily comings and goings of the busy fishing fleet. If the fish aren't biting, you can always hop round the corner to Haven Fish & Chips for a meal of hot salty chips and battered warehou. While you're waiting, wander next door and have a look at the board in the window of Guyton's fish shop telling you what species the shop is selling that day. There's never an excuse for coming home empty-handed after a day's fishing down at the Port.

The harvesting of seafood has been an important activity in Tasman Bay since the beginning of human settlement in the region. Several large estuaries fed by rivers provide nutrients and nursery areas for the variety of fish and shellfish species that can be found in Tasman and Golden Bays. Eroding sand hills expose middens containing shell and the bones of fish, seals and birds. Stones used to weight kaharoa or beach seines in pre-European times have been found behind Rabbit Island. The fibre nets have long since rotted away but the pattern of the stones gives their purpose away. When James Cook travelled around the New Zealand coast he observed that the nets of the Maori 'were superior and the cordage equal in strength and evenness' to his own. Maori had become competent fishers through necessity as they had not found New Zealand well supplied with animal foods.

When European settlers began to arrive in New Zealand their primary concern was the acquisition and breaking in of land and the establishing of farms. These folk were not great fish eaters, for roads were few and the lack of refrigeration posed problems for preservation and storage. Fish had to be either eaten where and when it was caught or salted, smoked or dried for consumption later on. Mutton or beef, on the other hand, was cheaper, more widely available and could be kept live and fresh until required. As early as 1897, the then Leader of the Opposition was on record as saying, 'The poorer people… were not able to get enough fish as food at reasonable rates… in all the colonies there was too much meat eaten by children, and if there was more fish and porridge there would be less doctors' bills to pay'. But as roads and transport improved, fresh fish began to feature more frequently in the diet of New Zealanders. Fish and oyster saloons were to be found in most New Zealand towns until well into the 20th century and were places where diners could enjoy oyster stews and oysters on the shell as well as fish 'suppers' and lunches. Many Nelsonians will remember Peter's Fish Shop in Hardy Street, where there were always mutton birds and cooked crayfish in the window and wooden trays of pre-cooked fish fillets and chips under the counter.

The limitations on storing and transporting seafood meant that commercial fishing in New Zealand was slow to develop until refrigeration came to Nelson in 1900 when it was fish rather than meat that benefited initially. The Nelson Fishing Company formed in 1900 had, by 1901, installed freezing machinery at its new premises at the Port, but early commercial fishing efforts were small in scale by today's standards. There was conflict between the longline and seine net fishermen and those who employed a new method using the otter trawl. Trawling meant larger vessels and heavier gear and as oil-fired vessels became more efficient and began to replace coal-burning steamers, the industry started to expand slowly. From early in the twentieth century, exports of smoked, canned and frozen fish to Australia were on the increase. Now the seafood industry in Nelson contributes nearly one third of the city's GDP and its direct, indirect and induced contribution to the Nelson economy is illustrated by the fact that each job at sea generates almost eight jobs ashore.

Today we are much more aware of the variety of fish species which are available, the cooking methods and health benefits. This is partly due to generic industry promotion but also because of the efforts of seafood companies and processors to promote particular species. The greenshell mussel and king salmon are two good local examples. Add to these our Tasman Bay scallops, dredge oysters, cockles and geoduck clams from Golden Bay, a range of succulent inshore fin-fish species and you start to understand why there is a seafood chowder on the menu of most Nelson restaurants. Match a seafood meal with a wine from one of the many excellent vineyards in the region and you'll have a dining experience that is hard to equal.

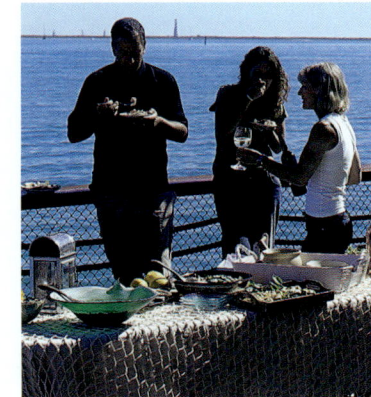

We need to become more aware of the seasonality of seafood if we want to eat it at its best. Generally, inshore species such as snapper and John Dory are at their best in the summer months. Fish from deeper waters reach their optimal condition in the winter. Seasonality has a direct influence on availability so don't expect your favourite fish to be on the menu all year round. That old phrase 'fish of the day' is a reflection on the season, weather, supply and price but it should be the best fish that the chef was able to source that morning. Fresh tuna, mussels, crayfish and salmon are available year round and so freshness shouldn't be a problem but for other species a chef needs to look around and use some local knowledge. For example, fresh turbot would have to be the fish of choice in Westport or Greymouth but is virtually unobtainable in Nelson. But try finding a meal of fresh snapper or John Dory on the West Coast. This is as it should be, each region having its own speciality and its own seasonal seafood choices.

Most of us would agree that the perfect seafood meal takes some beating and the wonderful thing is that this can take so many forms, from a fresh catch cooked over a driftwood fire on the beach, a pot of steaming greenshell mussels or a perfectly grilled fillet of white warehou or seared mahi-mahi served in more formal surroundings. In New Zealand it is still possible for us to go out and catch our own fish and perhaps this is part of the magic of our relationship with seafood. As long as we value and respect the seafood resource we have in New Zealand and especially here in Nelson, we will always have the ability to enjoy the experience of fishing and eating our catch in ever more creative and delicious concoctions.

Alec Woods

fresh nelson oysters mignonette

The best way to serve Nelson oysters is on the half shell. Here is a simple but delicious way of serving them from Michael Lawrence of Nelson's Oyster Bar.

1 cup balsamic vinegar
crushed ice
six fresh oysters per person

1 tablespoon minced spring onion per person
1 tablespoon caviar per person

Place the balsamic vinegar in a small saucepan and bring to the boil.

Boil gently until reduced to about a third of a cup and then set aside to cool.

When ready to serve, cover a large flat serving dish with crushed ice and arrange the oysters in the half shell on top.

Drizzle the reduced balsamic vinegar sparingly over the oysters.

Sprinkle with a little minced spring onion and caviar and serve immediately.

onekaka mussel chowder

This recipe is from the Mussel Inn at Onekaka in Golden Bay, famous for it's boutique brewery as well as its mussels.

150g onion, sliced
1 tablespoon olive oil
450ml water
75ml white wine
120g carrot, grated
300g potato, grated
120ml tasty tomato sauce
1 tablespoon fresh basil, chopped

½ teaspoon freshly ground black pepper
salt to taste (approximately 1 tablespoon)
1 teaspoon soy sauce
300g cooked mussel meat, roughly chopped
½ cup cream

Sauté the onion in a little oil.

Add the water, wine, carrot, potato, tomato sauce, basil, pepper, salt and soy sauce.

Simmer gently for approximately 15 minutes until the vegetables are tender.

Add the chopped mussel meat and heat through.

Put the soup in a blender or food processor and pulse briefly to thicken and blend flavours.

Stir in most of the cream and adjust the salt if necessary.

Pour into bowls, top with a swirl of the remaining cream, and serve with fresh crusty bread.

kedgeree stuffed capsicums

Originating with the British Army in India this dish was served from the sideboard at breakfast time, alongside kidneys and mushrooms. Today we eat kedgeree as a supper dish and here it is adapted for outdoor eating by serving it in cooked capsicum halves.

1 tablespoon butter
2 medium onions, finely chopped
1 large clove garlic, finely chopped
180g basmati rice
¼ cup verjuice or white wine
500mls stock (a tetrapak of fish or chicken stock is fine)
300g smoked fish, cut into bite sized pieces
2 teaspoons tumeric

½ teaspoon ground cumin
½ teaspoon curry powder
½ teaspoon salt
½ teaspoon cracked pepper
3 hard boiled eggs, roughly chopped
2 spring onions, chopped
a handful of fresh parsley, chopped
1 tablespoon lemon juice
3 large red capsicums
lemon or lime wedges to serve

Melt the butter in a large saucepan, add the onions and garlic and cook gently until soft. Add the rice and continue cooking until the rice softens a little and starts to look translucent.

Add the verjuice or wine, the stock, smoked fish, spices and salt and pepper.

Stir to thoroughly combine, cover with a lid and cook gently until the rice is tender – about 10-15 minutes. Add more stock if necessary to keep the rice moist.

When the rice is cooked stir in the eggs, spring onions, parsley and lemon juice.

Slice the capsicums in half lengthwise and remove the seeds and ribs.

Fill the capsicum halves with kedgeree, place on an oiled baking tray and cover with foil. Bake at 180°C for 15 minutes.

Serve warm or cold with lemon or lime wedges.

This recipe is also good with finely sliced kaffir lime leaves or chopped coriander replacing the parsley.

kina beach kokoda

Kokoda (pronounced 'kodonda') originates in Fiji, but works beautifully with some of the firm fleshed fish such as warehou and groper which are found in Tasman Bay.

1kg very fresh firm fish fillets such as warehou, cut into 1.5 cm cubes
approximately 2 cups lemon juice
2 large red onions, chopped
1 red pepper, finely chopped
2 tomatoes, chopped
1 400ml can coconut cream

½ chilli, deseeded and chopped very fine
1 teaspoon salt
freshly ground black pepper
chopped chives
1 head of lettuce

Put the fish into a tallish glass or plastic bowl, cover with lemon juice and mix well. Refrigerate for 12 hours, stirring occasionally to ensure that the lemon juice and fish are well mixed.

When the fish has turned white throughout, drain off the lemon juice and mix the fish with the onions, red pepper, tomatoes, coconut cream, chilli, salt, pepper and chives.

Serve on a bed of lettuce with lots of fresh crusty bread to mop up the sauce.

boathouse smoked fish salad

Firm fresh Nelson fish such as snapper, blue nose, warehou or tuna is ideal for smoking. If you don't have a fish smoker you can smoke fish and other foods in a wok. Line a wok with heavy foil, scrunching up the edges so that you have a basin of foil in the base.

Place the manuka sawdust on top of the foil and cover with a round trivet or wire tray on which you have placed the marinated fish.

Cover with a tight fitting lid, place over a gas burner and proceed as outlined below.

1kg very fresh firm fish fillets
½ cup brown sugar
⅓ cup sea salt
¼ cup maple syrup

¼ cup soy sauce
½ cup boiling water
1 sheet heavy foil
1 cup untreated manuka sawdust

Prepare the fish fillets by cutting into pieces about 100g each.

Mix the brown sugar, sea salt, maple syrup, soy sauce and boiling water in a bowl to form a thick dark brine.

Pour the marinade onto a flat tray and lay the fish pieces in it for 30 minutes, turning every 10 minutes to make sure they are well infused.

Line the smoker with heavy foil and sprinkle manuka sawdust on top.

Insert the fish rack about 50 mm above the sawdust.

Pat the fish pieces dry with kitchen paper and place on the wire rack.

Light the gas or meths burners under the fish smoker and place the lid over the top once the smoking starts. Allow 15 minutes to cook the fish.

When the fish is smoked, break it into flakes and serve it on top of two cups of mesclun salad leaves garnished with chopped carrot, tomato, red onion, roast peppers, capers and lemon slices, all sprinkled with your favourite salad dressing.

The flaked fish is also delicious stirred into a mixture of tangy barbecue sauce and whipped cream and served on a bed of salad as above.

nelson flounder parcels

These flounder look stunning with the light and dark skinned fillets arranged in an attractive pattern in the baking dish. Vogel's bread is a heavy grained bread made in New Zealand.

4 slices Vogel's bread, toasted
½ red capsicum, finely chopped
4 medium ripe tomatoes, finely chopped
2 small zucchini, finely chopped
1 medium red onion, finely chopped
2 tablespoons chives, finely chopped
½ teaspoon black pepper

¾ teaspoon salt
50g Parmesan cheese, coarsely grated
14 small flounder fillets (with mixed light and dark skins)
a little finely ground Parmesan cheese to finish

Chop the bread in a food processor, add the capsicum, tomatoes, zucchini, onion, chives, black pepper, salt and Parmesan cheese and whiz briefly to mix.

Adjust seasoning to taste, spoon mixture onto flounder fillets and roll up so that the skin is on the outside.

Place the stuffed fillets in a shallow greased oven dish, creating a pattern with the white and grey skins of the flounder fillets.

Spoon any remaining stuffing around the fillets where there are spaces in the dish.

Sprinkle a little finely ground Parmesan cheese on top and bake at 180°C for about 40 minutes or until the top has toasted brown.

Serve with steamed vegetables or a green salad.

brujdet

This recipe and the one which follows were brought to New Zealand by Ivan Talley when he came from Igrane, Croatia. They have been family favourites for four generations.

3 large onions, finely chopped
3 teaspoons garlic, crushed
3 tablespoons olive oil
8 large tomatoes, skinned and chopped
1 tablespoon tomato paste

1kg snapper fillets (or any firm fish)
2 tablespoons vinegar
2 tablespoons white wine
2 teaspoons salt
1 teaspoon sugar

Sauté the onion and garlic in olive oil until soft.

Stir in the tomatoes and tomato paste and continue to cook for about three minutes

Cut the snapper fillets into bite sized pieces and add along with vinegar, wine, salt and sugar.

Continue to cook over a low heat until the fish is cooked through. Do not allow the mixture to boil.

Remove from the heat, cool and chill in the refrigerator before serving.

blitva

1kg potatoes, peeled and cut into small pieces
1kg silverbeet

2 cloves garlic, finely chopped
¼ cup olive oil
2 teaspoons salt

Boil the potatoes in salted water until tender. Drain very well and mash.

Steam the silverbeet, drain and chop finely.

Add the silverbeet, garlic, olive oil and salt to the mashed potatoes and mix well.

paua fritters

These paua fritters are light and delicious. Serve them immediately with a fresh green salad sprinkled with a lemon vinaigrette.

5 paua
1 medium onion
4-5 bacon rashers
salt and pepper

2 eggs
½ cup flour
1-2 tablespooons oil or butter
lemon wedges to serve

Clean the paua by washing in fresh water. Cut the teeth out of each mouthpiece and remove the sac. Mince the paua, onion, bacon rashers and one paua sac.

Season the mixture with salt and pepper. Beat the eggs and stir in a half cup of sifted flour. Mix well with the paua mixture.

Heat a fry pan and add oil or butter. Drop tablespoons of the fritter mixture into the pan and cook for two minutes on each side.

Serve with wedges of lemon and a seasonal salad.

boutique brews

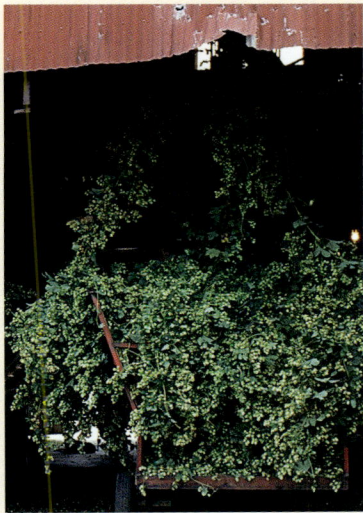

Drive around the German settlement of Upper Moutere in the summer and you will see many hectares of land sprouting huge wooden poles hung with wire and carrying bright green plants which grow vigorously up entwined strings. These are some of Nelson's hop gardens and they are a unique feature of our rural landscape. Nelson is the only region in New Zealand which grows hops commercially and we've been at it for more than 100 years. The hop drying kilns, with their distinctive pitched roofs, were a favourite subject of Nelson artists John Hoyte, Mina Arndt and Toss Woollaston, and it is fortunate this legacy exists in their paintings as so few of the original oast houses are left now.

Follow a laden hop truck swaying down Old House Road or up the Supplejack Valley in early March and the sweet, soporific smell of ripe hops permeates the air. Walk into a hop kiln during drying time and stagger up flights of old wooden steps and your head will grow heavy. Trudge up each flight until at the top, in the semi-dark, the aroma becomes so powerful and the atmosphere so sticky you wonder how anyone can work in it. Layers of wire mesh racks are spread with thousands of cones which are gently dried until they are conveyed to the packing area where ancient presses hold sacks that are filled to bursting point. The hops are then transported to the New Zealand Hops coolstores in Appleby for processing and distribution. Modern equipment has been introduced to make the harvesting and processing more efficient, but there remains a sense of the history of the industry with hops still picked in pecks and the knives used to cut them from the strings traditionally called 'cats'.

It is said that Captain Cook was the first to brew beer in New Zealand, in 1770 at Dusky Sound in Fiordland. Of course, he had no hops at hand so he flavoured his beer with rimu and manuka both of which, like hops, contain tannins, terpenes, ellagic acid and diterpenoids, and have medicinal qualities.

Hops contain both an antiseptic and a preservative. The famous India Pale Ale was characteristically heavily hopped to provide the longevity required to make the arduous journey by sea from the English brewers to the British colonists in India. The first ever food purity laws, the Reinheitsgebot, which originated in Bavaria in 1516, specified that beer must contain only four ingredients: water, malted barley, yeast and hops. Whilst most commercially produced beers now contain additives such as sugar, flaked maize and even rice, nearly all of them continue to use hops in one form or another. Hops help clarify the wort (the malt and sugar solution), provide a good head, improve the keeping qualities of the beer and give it that characteristic bitter flavour and aroma. The hop plant, *humulus lupulus*, is a fast growing, perennial, twisting vine that needs plenty of moisture in spring and warm sunny summers. The exact origin of *humulus lupulus* is unknown, but it grows best in deep, well-drained, loamy soil, with little or no wind, and on a flat site to aid the harvesting of the cone-shaped female flowers from the tall vines. Much of the Nelson region has just these attributes, with some 350 hectares planted in hop gardens on flat plains and river terraces at Riwaka, Upper Moutere and Tapawera.

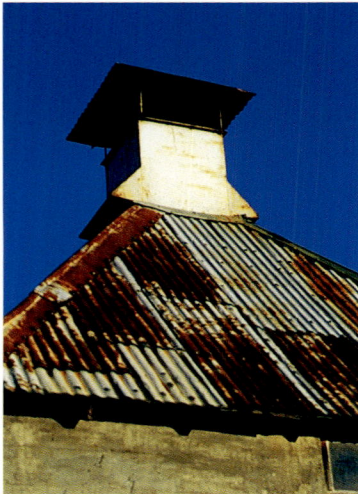

New Zealand produces some 800,000kg of hops annually which are sold as cones (flowers), pallets and extract. Over 80% is exported to the UK, Europe, the USA, Japan, India and South East Asia. This provides northern hemisphere brewers with access to fresh hops during the winter season when the quality of stored hops is declining. The New Zealand industry can also boast a very low need for the application of pesticides and this is increasingly attractive to consumers the world over.

The New Zealand hop industry has benefited enormously from improved hop cultivars developed by HortResearch, a Government owned research institute in Nelson. Over the years New Zealand scientists have led the world in developing new hop varieties including cultivars which are resistant to *phytophthora* (which once threatened to destroy the local industry) and varieties with a very high bittering content – the latter a mixed blessing as fewer hops are now needed to flavour the beer!

The availability of locally grown hops, along with a regional disposition towards culinary creativity, has spawned a thriving brewing industry in Nelson. The combination of spring water, malt, yeast and hops blended in traditional, and increasingly innovative, recipes lend diverse regional flavours to a brew and local brewers have turned this to advantage. There is a long tradition of brewing here with the first brewery being established in 1842 by Thomas Renwick and Charles Hooper. By 1872 the region boasted seven breweries, with many profiting handsomely from the gold rushes when thousands of prospectors and miners arrived in search of wealth, and pubs became the cornerstone of social activities.

In Nelson there are six boutique breweries which are well respected internationally. The Duncan family has been involved in brewing since 1854 and six generations have served as maltsters, hop growers and general importers. John Duncan, with his sons Callum, Sholto and Matt, operates Founders Brewery, Nelson's only organic brewery, set in the extensive grounds of Founders Historic Park in Atawhai. Organic hops are sourced from nearby Tapawera and malt is brought in from Canterbury and Germany. Founders' three lagers and one ale are exported worldwide as well as being very popular with Nelsonian's own discerning palates. Founders' Long Black beer makes a perfect combination with the walnuts in our walnut and black beer baps, and is an excellent accompaniment to the beef carbonade.

The Mussel Inn at Onekaka in Golden Bay is renowned for a superb selection of local beers, and the scenic drive through Riwaka's hop gardens and across the Takaka Hill certainly helps work up a thirst. The Mussel Inn produces startlingly good beers, such as their Golden Goose Lager and Dark Horse, using both organic hops and home-grown hops from the beer garden in front of the Inn. Their Captain Cooker Manuka Beer uses fresh manuka tips to flavour the brew and has a wonderful and distinctly New Zealand flavour. Captain Cooker was the only beer of 240 New Zealand beers to rate 10 out of 10 in Keith Stewart's book *The Complete Guide to New Zealand Beer*. As well as beer, the Mussel Inn produce their own cider, home-made lemonade and ginger beer.

Nelson also boasts the country's smallest brewery – Dick Tout's Lighthouse Brewery – named after the Nelson harbour lighthouse that stands majestically on the Boulder Bank. Originally a home brewer of some repute, and still brewing in just 200 litre batches, Dick now single-handedly produces a range of beers from a subtle chocolatey stout to a delicately hopped pilsner. His beers have won many awards, including a silver medal at the 2002 Australian International Beer Awards for the Tasman Bay Pilsener. Dick's Dark (named after himself!) and his Classic Stout both won bronze medals at the same event. Haulashore Bitter (named after Haulashore Island in Nelson harbour) is also a local favourite.

Yet another multi-award winner is Nelson Bays Brewery in Stoke - their outstanding Bay's Gold Lager was judged best New Zealand lager for 2003/2004. Bays also produce their own version of India Pale Ale, Bengal Bitter, a heavily hopped beer with a nose to match.

Craig Harrington's brewery in Richmond has achieved international fame as the brewer of the Sobering Thought Ale for the Prancing Pony pub in the first Lord of the Rings movie, *The Fellowship of the Ring*. Craig and his head brewer Paul Cooper make their beers on the malty side and their wheat beer is one of the best. Harrington's boast some 11 whole malt beers with more in the pipeline, and if you visit the brewery Craig is always happy to provide a taste of his latest brew.

McCashin's Brewery and Malthouse, known by everyone as 'Macs Brewery', was started in 1981 by ex-All Black Terry McCashin. Now owned by Lion Nathan, the bulk of their famous Mac's Gold production is based in Auckland, but their craft beers are still made in Nelson and take advantage of the pure spring water available on the brewery site. As well as their range of all-malt ales and lagers Mac's produce cider and ginger beer and run daily tours of their Stoke brewery.

It is clear that Nelsonian's are spoiled for choice when it comes to beer, but it is not just the quality and variety of the local boutique brews which are surprising. The industry is full of colourful and interesting characters who make a tour of the boutique breweries a delightful experience – especially on a typically hot Nelson day when a cold beer or two at the source of production is just the ticket.

Martin Townshend

cherry tomato and feta tarts

The sharp flavour of these tarts would sit well with a long cool lager from one of Nelson's boutique breweries.

one large bunch fresh basil
1 cup olive oil
½ teaspoon sea salt
½ teaspoon freshly ground
black pepper

40-45 cherry tomatoes
250g fresh feta cheese
6 individual tart shells made from
home made or frozen savoury short
crust pastry and baked blind

Wash the basil and place 30-35 leaves in a saucepan with the olive oil.

Bring to the boil, turn off the heat, cover and leave to infuse overnight.

The next day chop another 10-15 basil leaves and place in a clean jar with the strained olive oil (reserving the cooked basil leaves).

Add the salt and pepper to the jar and shake to combine.

Just before serving, assemble the tarts as follows.

Brush the tomatoes with a little of the oil and grill briefly to soften. Cut the feta cheese into chunks about the same size as the tomatoes.

Arrange the cooked basil leaves in the pastry bases and arrange the feta and tomatoes on top.

Spoon a little basil oil over each tart and decorate with fresh basil leaves.

Any remaining basil oil can be stored in the refrigerator and used in salad dressings or marinades.

walnut and black beer baps

These baps are quick and easy to make. They are wonderful with blue cheese and are ideal to mop up the gravy of beef carbonade.

1 medium onion, chopped
4 tablespoons olive oil
4 cups strong white flour
3 teaspoons brown sugar
1 teaspoon salt
1 tablespoon active dried yeast
2 teaspoons bread improver

1 cup Founders Long Black beer
(or other dark beer)
1 cup boiling water
1 cup rye flour
¾ cup walnuts, chopped
¼ cup fresh rosemary, chopped

Fry the onion gently in one tablespoon of the olive oil until translucent. Mix two cups of the white flour, sugar, salt, yeast, and bread improver in a large mixing bowl.

Pour the beer and the boiling water on top of the flour mixture, add the warm onions and stir until well mixed.

Sprinkle one more cup of white flour, the rye flour and the walnuts on top and leave for five minutes to activate the yeast.

Meanwhile add the rosemary and three more tablespoons of olive oil to the onion pan, stir to blend the flavours and then pour most of the oil and rosemary on top of the flour mixture. Brush a large baking tray with more of the oil and set in a warm oven to heat the tray. Sprinkle the remaining cup of white flour onto a clean bench.

Mix the dough ingredients together briefly and turn onto the floured bench. Knead for five minutes, incorporating the flour, and until the dough feels elastic (if it is sticky add a little more flour). Cut the dough into 8-10 pieces, roll into balls, dust with flour, and flatten to form bap shapes approximately 15mm thick.

Remove the warm tray from the oven, place the baps on the tray, and brush with any remaining oil and rosemary mixture. Cover with a clean tea towel and leave in a warm place until doubled in size (approximately half an hour).

Heat the oven to 180°C, place the tray in the oven and raise the temperature to 220°C. Fan bake for 15 minutes or until lightly browned. As soon as the tray is removed from the oven, flip each bap over and allow to cool upside down (this helps keep the underside crisp). These baps freeze well either before or after they are cooked.

mussels cooked in pale ale

A delectable way to enjoy Nelson mussels; the ale adds an unusual twist to the flavours.

70g butter
2 red onions, finely chopped
2 cloves garlic
1 teaspoon fresh thyme, finely chopped
400ml pale ale
4 tablespoons Italian parsley,
finely chopped

pinch of salt
pinch of sugar
freshly ground pepper to taste
2kg clean mussels

Melt butter in a pan and sauté the onions and garlic until soft.

Add thyme, pale ale, half the parsley, salt, sugar and pepper.

Simmer for five minutes, strain, and return the liquid to the pan.

Bring to the boil, add mussels, cover and boil until the mussels open (discarding any mussels which do not open).

Remove the mussels to a deep bowl and keep warm.

Add the remainder of the parsley to the liquid in the pan, boil until reduced a little, pour over the mussels, and serve with wholemeal bread.

beef carbonnade

This dish is a great winter warmer. Highly recommended!

3 tablespoons olive oil
1 large onion, finely chopped
1kg braising steak, cut into large cubes
2 cups dark beer
2 teaspoons French mustard
2 teaspoons brown sugar

2 teaspoons malt vinegar
1 bay leaf
1 teaspoon fresh thyme, chopped
1 teaspoon salt
freshly ground black pepper
50g fresh rye breadcrumbs

Heat the oven to 180°C.

Heat the oil in a flameproof casserole dish over a moderate heat.

Add the onion and gently fry for five minutes until soft and translucent.

Add the beef and fry for five minutes, turning frequently, until brown on all sides.

Stir in the beer, mustard, sugar, vinegar, bay leaf, thyme, salt and pepper, and bring to a simmer.

Cover and place in the oven for two hours or until the beef is tender.

Remove from the oven and stir in the breadcrumbs.

Taste, adjust the seasoning, and remove the bay leaf before serving.

jerusalem artichokes with bacon

These little root vegetables have a delicious smoky flavour and make a beautiful soup. They are a devil to peel, unless you can get them freshly dug. However they are worth the effort and this simple dish is impressive and goes well with a dark ale.

500g Jerusalem artichokes, peeled
rock salt
2 tablespoons fresh parsley, finely chopped

1 tablespoon olive oil
100g of the very best streaky bacon or pancetta, chopped
3 tablespoons breadcrumbs

Boil the artichokes in salted water until just tender, drain and add freshly ground salt and parsley.

Heat the oil in a frying pan, add the bacon or pancetta, and fry until crisp and brown.

Transfer the bacon to kitchen paper to remove most of the fat. Add the breadcrumbs to the hot pan and fry until golden brown. Return the artichokes and bacon to the pan, toss quickly with the breadcrumbs, and transfer to a warm platter.

Add a little more chopped parsley and salt if desired.

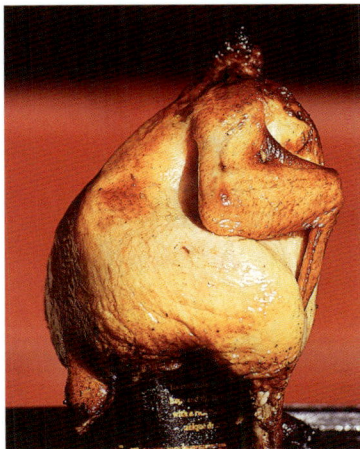

chooks on a can

This recipe is like an urban myth – everyone has heard the story but can't remember where it came from or if it is real.

It is an easy way to feed a hungry crowd – you can cook as many chickens as your barbecue will handle. It isn't just tender and tasty; if the conversation starts to wane just lift the lid on your barbecue and wait for the chortling. These quantities are for a single fowl – to feed about six people. It really does need a barbecue with a hood.

1 can of the best beer you have on hand
1 tablespoon chopped garlic
1 tablespoon chopped green ginger
handful of fresh herbs (eg parsley, basil, thyme), finely chopped

cooking oil
1 size 14 chicken
salt and pepper

Heat the barbecue. Open the can of beer and drink half of it.

Add the garlic, ginger and herbs to the half full can and add oil until the can is nearly full. Take the chicken, sit it on top of the can, and push down until the can is scarcely visible. Rub more oil over the outside of the chicken and rub with salt and pepper.

Put the chicken sitting on its beer can throne on the barbecue, lower the hood and cook for ¾-1 hour or until the juices run clear.

During the cooking time check to see it isn't browning too fast.

mac's black and beef pies

Perfect pies for the boys – dark, tangy and tasty.

300g parsnips
1 tablespoon olive oil
500g good quality stewing steak, diced
½ bottle Mac's Black ale
1 small onion, chopped
½ teaspoon freshly ground black pepper
1 teaspoon sugar
1 tablespoon whole grain mustard
1 small bouquet garni (1 bay leaf tied
together with 3 sprigs of thyme)

¼ cup flour mixed to a smooth paste
with ¼ cup cold water
salt
650g savoury shortcrust pastry
500g flaky pastry
1 egg beaten with 1 tablespoon water
or milk to glaze

Peel parsnips and cut into 1.5cm cubes.

Toss with olive oil and roast in a hot oven for 30 minutes, turning once during cooking.

Meanwhile place beef, Mac's Black, onion, pepper, sugar, mustard and bouquet garni into a heavy based saucepan.

Cover with a tight fitting lid and bring to the boil.

Reduce the heat to the lowest possible setting and cook, just simmering, for 45 minutes.

Add roasted parsnip cubes and continue cooking over a low heat, checking every 15 minutes, until beef is tender.

Remove from the heat, stir in the flour paste, and bring back to the boil, stirring until the sauce thickens. Add salt to taste and set aside to cool.

Roll out the shortcrust pastry to three mm thick and line six individual pie dishes with a nine cm diameter. Fill with cold beef mixture.

Cut lids from the flaky pastry, rolled to three mm thick.

Brush edges of pie bases with cold water and press the lids down on top.

Cut a small hole in the top of each pie to release steam while cooking and refrigerate pies for 10 minutes. Meanwhile heat oven to 200°C.

Brush tops of pies with egg glaze and bake for 40 minutes or until the pastry is golden brown.

tamarillo tart

The sharpness of the tamarillos in this recipe is beautifully balanced by the sweet almond sponge. Good served with ice cream accompanied by cider, homemade lemonade or a light ale.

shortcrust pastry to line a 23cm pie dish
125g butter
125g caster sugar
2 eggs
150g ground almonds

45g flour
½ teaspoon almond essence
10 tamarillos
½ cup sugar
2 tablespoons butter

Pre-heat the oven to 190°C.

Roll the pastry to four mm thick, line the pie dish and trim the edges of the pastry.

Cream the butter and caster sugar in a food processor until light and fluffy.

Add the eggs and process until well mixed. Add the ground almonds, flour and almond essence and process for a few seconds more.

Spread the almond mixture over the bottom of the pastry shell.

Plunge tamarillos into boiling water for 10 seconds, drain and peel.

Cut each tamarillo in half lengthways and arrange on top of the almond mixture cut sides down. Sprinkle with the sugar and dot with butter.

Bake on the lowest oven shelf for 45 minutes or until lightly browned and set.

Serve warm or at room temperature.

to market, to market

To market, to market…this is what the people of Nelson do every Saturday throughout the year. The dawn has not even hit the sky in the winter; six am, when the air speaks of snow on Mt Arthur and the trucks, trailers, utes, and hand pushed carts roll into Montgomery Square in downtown Nelson. Tables are set out, poles clink as awnings rise, gas burners roar and a coffee smell drifts through the strengthening light. Fresh vegetables are pulled from trucks and vans, are spread in boxes and bunches, this stall in a U shape, that one a strong middle block with side corridors, a third a small table facing out into the walkway. Stall holders in wool beanies and gloves greet neighbours, perch on the back of their vans with a thermos of coffee, or make their way to the end stall where the first blue enamel coffee pot of the day has been filled. This early readiness is in contrast to the first Nelson market. In 1860 *The Colonist* reported, 'The hour for opening was fixed at eight o'clock, but this was an erroneous calculation, for it is well known that Nelson folks do not think of commencing business so soon in the morning; and consequently, although patrons with their market baskets were waiting for the gates to be opened it was near ten o'clock before many of the stalls were occupied.'

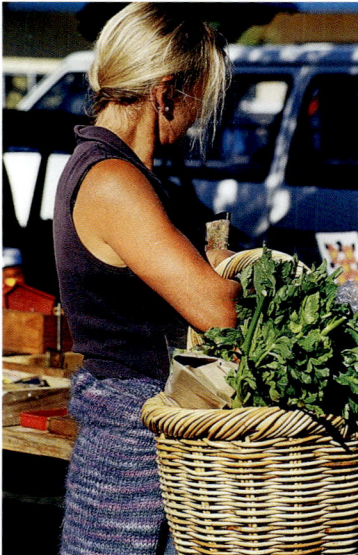

Nelson has a long history of markets. In pre-European times Maori would camp at Auckland Point, sharing food from cultivations on the south side of the Maitai River, and eels from the serpentine eel pond which is now the lake in Queen's Gardens. The 1842 Tuckett's Plan of Nelson Town shows an area set aside around the eel pond for a meat market and other areas were assigned for fish and cattle markets.

In contrast to the first Nelson market, the present market does start successfully by eight am. Before seven thirty the first shoppers arrive, scouting for the freshest, the greenest, the cheapest or the most unusual. They carry their own well-worn shopping bags and make the rounds of their favourite stalls. Doris, who sells a variety of German sausages and salamis, leaves home by five am each Saturday to be ready for her customers. The first are usually other stall holders who come to her for a breakfast of traditionally made bratwurst served on a fresh bread roll with imported European mustard and juicy sauerkraut. Doris is a firm believer in being at the market each week, rain or shine. From small beginnings in 1992 Doris has built her business into a thriving success. She learned her trade apprenticed to a butcher in Bavaria, and still imports spices and sausage casings so that her sausages are true to type. Sausage and roll in hand, Doris' customers sit at a nearby picnic table, enjoying the sun and the music and often adding to the market's international flavour by talking in German or Japanese or Mandarin.

On the next aisle over you can usually find Poppy, pressing samples of her many pear varieties onto her customers. From January to November she is there each week, selling large amounts of pears at each market. Before buying you are encouraged to sample, and to identify what sort of pear appeals to you most. A young man turns up who wants pears suitable for cooking with lamb and rosemary (she recommends full-flavoured Winter Coles) and the next woman wants pears as crisp as apples (for this Poppy fills a bag with Twyford's Monarch, a pear which she has developed into a commercial crop propagating from just one original tree). Part of Poppy's vision is to preserve the older varieties so that they don't get lost as new commercial varieties appear.

The market owes its existence to Nita Knight. Back in 1979 Nita approached the Nelson City Council with a proposal to operate an open air Saturday market in a public car park in the Nelson city centre but it took over three years before the market gained a team of regular stallholders and strong weekly patronage from the local community. Nita has a strong philosophy on what makes a good market. For her, products need to be local, but that can mean cherries from Marlborough or jams and chutneys from Moutere Gold or crafts from the rimu-rich West Coast. Products that come onto the market are chosen carefully and stalls are placed to complement each other, scattering vegetables, jewellery, wooden platters, flowers and used household items among baked goods, hot food, plant and soap stalls. One of the market's great charms is a pervasive feeling of whimsy. There are fairy dresses, possum puppets, airplanes made from recycled beer tins, wheat grass beads, yellow ceramic gumboots. Local theatre groups troop through in costumes, buskers create slow-motion sculptures and kilted pipe bands march in step. To Nita the market is a mirror of everything that is special in the region. 'It is a place where people of all ages buy, sell, laugh, meet and mingle. It is a real market that spills people on into town feeling good and part of this unique little community. I am delighted with the market and what it brings to the community of Nelson. It is on track with the vision I had when I started out, but there will never be a completion point; it is ever changing', she says. Hurrying is not something most people do at the market. The pace is relaxed, friendly and inclusive; stallholders love to chat rather than just making a quick sale. Most genuinely love talking about their product, explaining how it is made or its history. They enjoy the interface of knowing who is using their goods, and getting feedback on what they like or dislike. The contact creates a bond between buyer and seller, often a bond which lasts many years – no warehouse or supermarket intervenes in the process. More and more the market has become a Saturday morning meeting place for friends who gather at their favourite spot for coffee and *oliebollen* (delicious Dutch apple donuts), Asian stir fries, pancakes, chicken satay, falafel or sausages. Nearby cafes do a brisk trade as well, as marketgoers come and go, or choose to take a break from their buying. The market changes with the seasons. In spring flowers abound: roses, lisianthus, freesias, peonies, lily of the valley stand beside baby carrots, new potatoes, spring onions, and fresh new lettuces. In summer the aisles can get gridlocked as tourists examine pottery, pick up wooden bowls, try on jewellery. The sunhat stall does a roaring trade and the fresh fruit ice cream line snakes down the walkway between the stalls. In autumn the crowds of tourists start to disappear, pumpkin, beans, tomatoes, red peppers and basil are plentiful and purple gentians stand next to red and gold chrysanthemums at the flower stalls. A rainy winter Saturday may start with some empty stall spaces; regulars arrive later, greet each other and step around puddles on their way to choosing mustard, fresh rocket, pears or organic tamarillos.

Wolfgang Mann has had an organic stall for fifteen years and has made organics an important attraction for marketgoers. Since his first market in November 1989 his staff haven't missed a Saturday. He stocks a full range of vegetables, fruit and eggs and customers are happy to line up for kiwifruit, cauliflower, half metre long daikon, juicy carrots as well as a variety of healthy greens. Another stall has organically farmed salmon from Marlborough, and George from Macedonia has limes, pumpkin, grapes, lemons, plums, grapefruit, and whatever vegetables might be in season. Brent Ferretti is famous for his broccoli and cos lettuces, and his willingness to sell basil, coriander and other herbs by weight is much appreciated. Some organic stallholders sell only one product on a seasonal basis: asparagus in spring, kumara or tamarillos in winter. As well as certified organic produce such as Wolfgang's there are a number of stalls boasting 'natural' or 'spray free' produce. Heath's Blueberries is one of these. Throughout the season they bring punnets of plump blueberries just begging to be taken home. Heath's produce is spray free, but they choose not to adhere to the rigorous programme needed for it to be certified organic.

At one o'clock stallholders start packing up. Meanwhile purchasers are making their way home with their bounty. Fruit bowls are being filled, flowers arranged, presents admired and wrapped ready for giving. In the afternoon some will play a 'new' CD from the music stall, or make spicy chestnuts, pear chutney or lime punch. In some houses the aroma of green curry or damson jam may drift through the air. It's been another satisfying and relaxing market Saturday.

Barbara Raeburn

lime punch

This punch is not for the fainthearted, but is a wonderful drink for the long summer evenings in Nelson.

½ cup sugar
1 cup warm water
2 cups white rum
juice of four limes
1 cup orange juice

crushed ice (put the cubes in a plastic bag and break up with a hammer if necessary)
slices of lime and mint for decoration

Put the sugar and warm water into a large jug and stir until the sugar is completely dissolved. Add the rum, lime juice and orange juice and refrigerate until very cold.
Take long glasses, half fill with crushed ice and add a slice of lime and a sprig of mint.
Fill the glasses with punch and… relax!

redwood valley spicy chestnuts

This simple recipe is a favourite of Redwood Valley chestnut growers Bill Page and Mary Heaphy and was sourced from a recipe book produced by the Chestnut Growers' Association.

chestnuts
2 teaspoons baking soda

grape seed oil
curry powder to taste

Place the chestnuts in a saucepan, cover with water and add the baking soda.
Boil the chestnuts for twenty minutes, drain and remove the shells.
Heat the oil and curry powder in a pan and sauté the chestnuts until coated and lightly browned.
Serve hot or cold, as a snack or starter to a meal. They are utterly delicious!

appleby pesto

Fresh walnuts are almost always available at the Market and are quite different to imported nuts which are often rancid.
Combined with fresh basil they make an excellent pesto which can be spread on crackers or fresh bread or mixed with pasta for a quick and tasty meal. In winter parsley can be substituted for the basil.

1 cup shelled fresh walnuts
2 large handfuls of fresh basil
2 large cloves garlic
1 teaspoon black pepper

1 teaspoon salt
¼ cup olive oil
¼ cup grated Parmesan cheese
1 teaspoon lemon juice

Chop the walnuts, basil and garlic together in a food processor.
Add the remaining ingredients and process until well mixed.

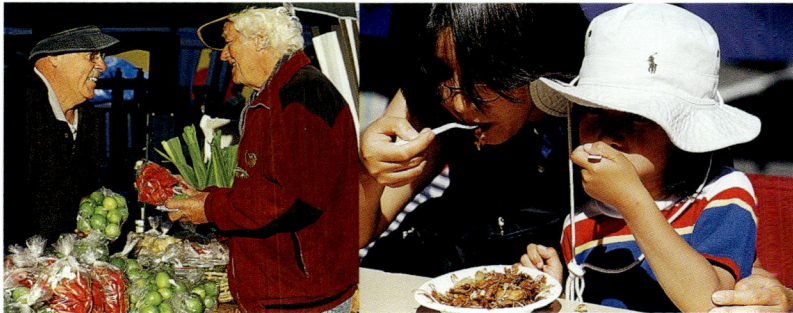

market green curry

The Vertu stall at the market sells a feast of tropical fruits and vegetables along with a delicious fresh green curry paste.

75g fresh Thai green curry paste (or commercial green curry paste)
500ml coconut milk
500g diced warehou or other firm fish
250g selected vegetables eg carrots, beans, zucchini or pumpkin cut into bite-sized pieces

60ml fish sauce
3 tablespoons sugar
200g diced aubergines – Japanese if possible
4 fresh Kaffir lime leaves
2 fresh Thai red hot chillies, deseeded (optional garnish)

Place the green curry paste into a wok or large saucepan over a medium heat and add the coconut milk.

Heat to boiling and add the diced fish, vegetables, fish sauce, sugar and aubergines, and bring back to the boil for two minutes.

Reduce the heat and simmer for approximately five minutes.

Add the Kaffir lime leaves.

Remove the contents to a serving bowl, garnish with sliced chilli and serve.

Serve with aromatic rice, with a finely chopped Kaffir lime leaf added to the rice as a garnish.

poppy's pear chutney

This chutney is a favourite of pear grower Poppy Dearbourn, and is delicious on French bread with feta cheese, or as an accompaniment to curry.

1 large onion
1 tablespoon salt
1.5kg Conference pears
300g white sugar
300ml cider vinegar

½ teaspoon curry powder
2 teaspoons hot English mustard powder
2 teaspoons wholegrain mustard
3 tablespoons plain flour

Peel and chop the onion, place in a bowl and sprinkle with salt. Cover, leave overnight and then drain. Peel and core the pears and cut into chunks.

Put pears into a large saucepan with the onion, sugar and half the vinegar.

Bring the mixture to the boil slowly, stirring well.

Reduce the heat and simmer for about twenty minutes or until the pears are soft, but not mushy. Remove from the heat.

Mix the curry powder, mustards and flour to a smooth paste with the rest of the vinegar. Add the paste to the pan stirring constantly, return to the heat and continue to cook for 10-15 minutes until the mixture is thick and almost transparent.

Allow to cool a little before packing into warm sterilised jars.

Seal and store for at least one month before using.

spicy blueberry sauce

In the unlikely event you have an excess of fresh blueberries, this makes an unusual sauce which is good to serve as an accompaniment to lamb, fish, or poultry.

2 cups blueberries
1 onion, peeled and chopped
½ cup sultanas or raisins
1 apple, peeled and chopped
1 cup cider vinegar

½ cup red wine
1-2 cloves garlic, crushed
1 bay leaf
1 teaspoon mustard seed
1 tablespoon brown sugar

Put all the ingredients in a saucepan and simmer for about 45 minutes.

Put the mixture through a Mouli or buzz in the food processor. Return to the saucepan and simmer for a few minutes more. Taste and add extra sugar if required.

Store in a sealed jar in the refrigerator.

daikon and carrot salad

This salad needs time for the flavours to meld, so it is best to make it the day before you want to serve it.

2 carrots
20cm daikon
I teaspoon salt

3 tablespoons caster sugar
70ml rice vinegar
1 tablespoon sesame seeds

Peel the carrots and daikon and julienne them or shred with a grater.

Put the vegetables into a bowl, sprinkle with the salt and mix well. Leave for 30 minutes and then drain well. Place vegetables into a clean bowl.

Mix the sugar and vinegar together until the sugar is completely dissolved and pour over the daikon and carrot. Leave for 24 hours mixing two or three times.

To serve pile onto a serving plate and sprinkle with sesame seeds.

kumara and tamarillo bake

Kumara is a tropical plant and ideally needs about five months of hot weather to mature. Kumara were grown by early Maori alongside the Waimea River where river stones kept the soil warm and extended the growing season.

6 kumara
1 tablespoon olive oil
1 teaspoon salt
pepper to taste

knob of butter
4 tamarillos
2 tablespoons brown sugar

Peel kumara and cut into four cm cubes.

Oven roast at 200ºC with a little olive oil and salt until soft.

Add pepper and a knob of butter to the kumara and mash coarsely with a fork.

While the kumara are roasting, pour boiling water over the tamarillos, leave for about 30 seconds to loosen the skin, then peel and chop them.

Mix the mashed kumara and the chopped tamarillos and place in a mound in an oiled baking dish.

Sprinkle the mound with the brown sugar.

Bake in a hot oven until caramelised, even a little burned.

Serve with steak, jus and green salad.

eggplant spread with north african seasoning

This delicious spread is best served at room temperature with roast vegetables or flatbread.

1 cup tamarind water (see below)
3 medium eggplants
½ cup olive oil
1 onion, finely chopped
4 cloves garlic, finely chopped

1 teaspoon cinnamon
2 teaspoons ground cumin
1 tablespoon smoked paprika
1 teaspoon brown sugar
salt and pepper to taste

To make the tamarind water, soak three tablespoons of tamarind in one cup boiling water for 10 minutes. Strain before using.

Cut the stems from the eggplants and slice into rounds one centimetre thick.

Fry these slices over a moderate heat using half the olive oil until golden brown.

Do this in batches, one layer at a time and turning once.

Drain the eggplant on kitchen paper and dice when cool.

Heat the remaining oil in the frying pan and sauté the onion until translucent.

Add the garlic, cinnamon, cumin, paprika and diced aubergine and sauté for 1-2 minutes until the mixture smells fragrant. Add the tamarind water and sugar and continue cooking over a gentle heat until the moisture is absorbed and the eggplant very soft. Mash roughly with a fork, season to taste and leave to cool.

fresh figs in balsamic vinegar

Ripe figs are very perishable; this recipe will extend their life. Serve with cheeses. They are also delicious served warm or cold as part of a salad entrée (tossed with olive oil and rocket).

8-10 fresh figs – halved
(use dried figs if fresh are not available)
¾ cup red wine
¼ cup balsamic vinegar

¼ cup runny honey
1 sprig rosemary or thyme
black pepper

Place wine, vinegar, honey and herbs in a pot and bring to the boil. Add figs and simmer until figs are tender.

Remove the figs into a bowl and simmer the syrup until it is reduced and slightly thickened. Pour syrup over the figs and top with a grind of black pepper.

damson jam with walnuts

This is a rich luxurious jam and the walnuts provide an unusual but interesting texture.

2kg damsons or other
dark fleshed plums
400g seedless raisins
2kg sugar

juice and grated rind of 2 oranges
juice and grated rind of 2 lemons
200g walnut halves

Crush the plums a little to help the juices flow. Remove any stones that come away easily and combine all ingredients with the exception of the walnuts in a preserving pan. Stir through and leave overnight.

Put the pan over a low heat and cook slowly until the sugar is completely dissolved.

Turn up the heat and boil until setting point is reached (when a skin quickly forms on a little jam dropped onto a cold plate). Skim jam and remove any remaining plum stones. Add the walnuts, pour into hot sterilised jars and seal.

afternoon tea on the orchard

Driving the coastal highway between Appleby and Motueka is a stunningly beautiful trip. Mountain and estuary vistas unfold as you navigate sweeping bends where apple orchards, vineyards, olive groves, and pine forests pattern the gently sculptured landscape. Clear Nelson light accentuates the forms created where ancient glaciers dumped moraine at the end of the last ice age. The hues are distinctly seasonal: verdant greens in winter, delicate touches of pink and white in spring, and earthy reds, golds and browns in summer and autumn. To live on an orchard is to appreciate the rhythms of nature, to marvel at how fruit can be kissed by the sun and flavoured by the earth. Tasting tree-ripened fruit is a culinary sensation that creates anticipation for every bite thereafter.

Without doubt the quality and variety of the fruit grown in the Nelson region is extraordinary. Apples, pears, grapes for wine production, a multitude of berries - blackcurrants, raspberries, blueberries, boysenberries and more – have been joined by more recent plantings of olives grown for the production of gourmet oils. Golden Bay, with its sheltered micro-climate, produces subtropical fruits such as citrus, tamarillo, passionfruit and avocado. For the gardener the regional climate provides fantastic growing conditions, and it is common for the home garden or farmlet to host quinces, persimmons, mulberries, feijoas, plums, apricots, nectarines, peaches, lemons, oranges, limes, walnuts, hazelnuts and chestnuts.

Wairepo, the venue for our afternoon tea party, is an orchard property that overlooks the estuary at Mariri, just past the little township of Tasman. Here the road finally straightens out, and runs along a causeway built to bypass the numerous little bays and inlets as you come into Motueka. Four generations of the Easton family have tended the orchards at Wairepo. The first orchard was planted in 1909 on 42 acres by William Bolt Easton who broke in land covered by scrubby fern and manuka. The main apple varieties planted then were Cox's Orange Pippin, Sturmer, Worcester, Delicious, Jonathan, Northern Spy and Dougherty along with Winter Nellis pears. Those early days were tough, as the pioneering efforts were interrupted by World War I. William was called to service and miraculously survived battles at Gallipoli in Turkey and at Paschendale and the Somme in France. The orchard was abandoned for the duration of the war when William's wife Hope returned to her family in the North Island.

Early orchard practice used horse-drawn farming equipment. At harvest time apples and pears were sized and graded by eye, wrapped in tissue paper and placed in wooden crates constructed of imported Oregon box timber. Stencils were used to brand and mark each box, before they were loaded onto horse drawn carts, and driven to the estuary jetty. They were barged to Motueka on the high tide, transferred to a coastal freighter and sent to Wellington to be sold on the local market. Hard times and heavy physical work prevailed.

Afternoon teas, tennis parties and packing shed dances were the predominant social activities. Memories of these occasions were vivid to some of the older guests who attended our tea party. Transport was difficult, and it was an all day affair to travel what would now be deemed a short trip. Frances Harris recalled riding her horse from Dehra Doon at the foot of the Takaka Hill to William and Hope's very sociable pre-war tennis parties. Refreshment stops were made on the way at friends' houses, and the ford at Lower Moutere was negotiated at low tide. With a wicked twinkle in her eye Frances spoke of the eligible bachelors she played tennis with, and the hilarious fun that was had with these same friends on hiking trips to the ranges around Mount Arthur.

Adele Robson recalled riding her bicycle from Riwaka during the war, over the bumpy metal roads that curved in and out the bays, to stay the weekend at Hope's. She remembers the afternoon teas of plump scones, home made raspberry jam, cucumber sandwiches and cream filled chocolate sponge cakes. Afternoon tea was a ritual, served on the wide veranda of the Easton's humble abode, or under trees in a garden spilling with fragrant roses. Three-quarter length dresses and straw hats trimmed with bright artificial flowers or cherries were the fashion of the day. William and Hope's only son Donald continued the orcharding tradition but his career was also interrupted with war service - this time in the Pacific between 1941 and 1944. After the war he extended the apple orchard with the acquisition of adjoining land.

By the late 1940s the industry had achieved much greater stability with the establishment of the New Zealand Apple and Pear Marketing Board. Collective marketing strength was established, and the use of resources was maximised with the coordination of packaging materials and cool storage facilities. Refrigerated shipping opened up worldwide export markets to New Zealand pipfruit growers and provided them with greater economic returns. Research was commissioned into new apple varieties and this proved to be a highly successful strategy. Hugely popular varieties such as Braeburn and Royal Gala were in fact sports

found on trees in Lower Moutere and Hawke's Bay respectively. Jazz (a cross between Braeburn and Royal Gala), Pacific Rose, and the red Braeburn sports Mariri Red and Mahana Red, Pink Lady (a Western Australian variety) and Fuji (a Japanese variety) added to the growing portfolio of New Zealand exports. By the 2004 season six and a half million cartons of pipfruit were exported from Nelson to Europe, the USA and Asia, but the industry was feeling the pressure of deregulation, the rise of the New Zealand dollar and increased shipping costs. Now there is a little more pessimism and uncertainty in the industry than in the days of the single desk marketing strategy of the Apple and Pear Board.

One interesting phenomenon generated by the establishment of the early Nelson pip fruit industry, was the planting of *pinus radiata* for box timber on adjoining hills that were unsuitable for orcharding. The forests planted by the Baigent family created a thriving new industry with sawmills popping up at Tasman, Motueka, Harakeke, Lower Moutere, Upper Moutere, Waiwhero, and Maisey's Road by the late 1950s. Forestry, like horticulture, remains to this day a mainstay of the regional economy, along with fishing and tourism.

Richard and Joyanne Easton, with their sons Simon and Matthew, now tend the Wairepo orchards, and have introduced new enterprises that complement the extensive orchard holdings. Peony flowers are grown commercially and Wairepo House hosts up to ten guests in an exclusive bed and breakfast style. The property still boasts a lawn tennis court and two acres of extensive gardens featuring stunning plantings of deciduous trees, roses and herbaceous borders, together with a swimming pool and play areas devoted to croquet and petanque. Abundant seasonal produce is the basis that Joyanne uses to treat guests with both traditional and modern regional cuisine. Apples are a staple and are used in a myriad of ways. Stewed apples, blended with rhubarb, blackcurrants or boysenberries, are popular served with breakfast pancakes, and fresh fruit salad is always a great favourite as well. Chutneys and pickles are one of Joyanne's specialities and their piquant flavours accompany locally smoked fish, meats, cheeses, and breads that are served off platters created by local artisans. Favourites include her pickled walnuts, feijoa chutney, quince paste and red pepper jam. Cakes, pies, scones and muffins are all livened up with the addition of seasonal fruits, and baking which traditionally has been served at afternoon tea time often appears for breakfast or dessert these days accompanied by home made raspberry and cranberry jam, lemon honey and orange and ginger marmalades.

Hospitality and simple pleasures still abound at Wairepo, as they do on many Nelson orchards. Seasonal rhythms of toil and leisure lead each year to the joy of reaping the harvest that nature serves up from the earth and to the pleasure of sharing that harvest around the orchard table!

Anne Rush

mariri fig and brown sugar tart

A delicious use for fresh figs in the autumn. However out of season you can make it with dried figs if you use the soft moist brands. It will not taste the same but it is still very good.

300g shortcrust pastry
3 egg whites
100g soft brown sugar
½ teaspoon almond essence

120g ground almonds (or ground walnuts or pecans)
as many figs as you fancy, halved or quartered

Roll out the pastry and line a greased 28cm loose-bottomed flan tin.
Beat the egg whites to soft peaks then gradually beat in most of the brown sugar to form a stiff meringue.
Fold in the almond essence and ground nuts.
Spread this mixture over the pastry base and arrange the sliced figs over the top.
Dust a little brown sugar over the top of each fig.
Bake at 200°C for 25-30 minutes until the tart is golden.
Stand for five minutes before cutting.
This tart is delicious hot or cold.

devonshire splits

Fruit jams are a must with these yeast based splits that originate from southern England and can be served with lashings of whipped cream.

25g fresh yeast (if possible use fresh yeast, otherwise substitute 12g dried yeast)
1⅓ cups tepid water
¼ cup melted butter, cooled
1 egg, beaten
4 cups high grade flour

¼ cup caster sugar
a good pinch of salt
2 teaspoons oil
1 egg yolk, beaten
2 tablespoons milk
icing sugar, cream and jam to serve

Place the yeast in a large bowl with the water and mix with a spatula.
Leave for 5-10 minutes until the yeast activates and starts to bubble.
Add the butter and the first beaten egg to the bowl and mix through.
Add the flour, sugar and salt to the yeast mixture, and mix to a smooth soft dough.
Knead for five minutes.
Smooth the top of the dough and brush with a little oil.
Cover and leave in a warm place for 1-1½ hours or until doubled in bulk.
Turn the dough onto a floured surface and knead well.
Divide the dough into twenty portions and form each into a flat bun shape.
Fold these in half so that the splits can be broken open when cooked, rather than cut.
Reshape into rounds and place on a greased baking tray. Brush the splits with the egg yolk and milk beaten together and leave for 20-30 minutes until nearly doubled in size.
Bake at 230°C for 10 minutes or until firm to the touch and pale in colour.
Dust with icing sugar and serve with bowls of whipped or clotted cream and fruit jam.

lavish plum, custard and almond cake

This delicious cake is filled with delectable dark plums and golden custard making it ideal for a special occasion. Home preserved Omega or Black Doris plums provide a wonderful flavour.

180g butter	2 cups self-raising flour
1 cup sugar	3 cups thick custard, cooled
1-2 drops almond essence	(homemade or use a tetrapak
4 eggs	from the supermarket)
½ cup plain yoghurt	2½ cups preserved dark red plums
½ cup milk	(or canned plums), drained
1 cup ground almonds	a little lemon icing or
½ cup semolina	icing sugar to finish

Cream the butter and sugar until fluffy and add the almond essence.

Beat in the eggs one at a time. Combine the yoghurt and milk and stir into the mixture.

Fold in the dry ingredients.

Grease or line a 24cm round springform cake tin.

Spread half the mixture across the bottom of the tin. Spoon the custard evenly over this. Place drained plums carefully across the top of the custard and top with the remaining cake mixture.

Bake at 180°C for approximately 50 minutes.

Leave in the tin to cool before removing.

Sprinkle with a little icing sugar or lightly drizzle with lemon icing.

raspberry and cranberry jam

A quickly made jam with a tantalising flavour.

500g raspberries	2 cups sugar
100g dried cranberries	½ cup water

Cover the cranberries with boiling water and set aside for 10 minutes.

Boil the sugar and water for five minutes.

Add the raspberries and drained cranberries to the sugar and water and boil for twenty minutes or until setting point is reached (ie a small amount dropped onto a cold plate will form a skin as it cools).

Pour into sterilised jars and seal, or serve immediately with Devonshire splits.

spiked pink ladies

Pink Lady is one of the newer varieties of apples that are available. Bred in Australia, they are renowned for their sweet flavour and crunchy texture and are sought after for both eating and baking. This recipe is a new take on a very traditional recipe.

'…comfort me with apples; for I am sick from love' (The Song of Solomon 2:5)

1¼ cups water
¾ cup sugar
juice of 1 lemon
4 even sized cooking apples
(Pink Ladies if possible)

approximately 50g pine nuts or
blanched almonds
quince jelly or paste

Place the water, sugar and lemon juice in a large saucepan and heat gently until the sugar is completely dissolved.

Peel and core the apples, and poach them gently in the sugar syrup until very nearly, but not quite tender.

Remove them carefully from the pan and stand them in an ovenproof dish.

Spike them all over with the pine nuts, or with slivers of almond, and spoon quince jelly or paste lavishly into the centres.

Reduce the syrup by boiling for a few minutes and baste the apples with it.

Bake the apples at 160ºC for ten minutes or until the apples are quite soft.

The apples can be served hot or cold. If they are to be served hot, stand them on circles of sponge cake fried golden and crisp in butter.

Just before serving pour a little thick cream over each one.

mahana microwaved quince paste

It is difficult to make quince paste by the traditional method without burning it. This method is much easier and makes a delicious paste which freezes well. Make sure you use a large bowl for cooking, otherwise the paste may overflow the container.

1kg quinces
500g sugar

juice of 1 lemon
1 cup water

Peel, core and chop the quinces into chunks and put in a large glass bowl with the lemon juice and half a cup of water. Cover with cling film and cook on high until the fruit is very mushy. Meanwhile, bring the sugar and half a cup of water slowly to the boil in a saucepan, stirring to dissolve the sugar. Simmer for 10 minutes.

Mash the fruit thoroughly (or whiz in the food processor until smooth) and mix with the sugar syrup in the glass bowl.

Microwave, uncovered, until the paste is very thick - about 40 minutes - stirring frequently. Wear oven gloves while doing this as the paste and the container will get very hot.

Spread in an oiled tray and allow to dry for three days in a warm place.

Cut into serving-size portions, wrap in cling film and store in the fridge or freezer.

Delicious with cold meats, cheese and crackers or antipasto platters.

panforte

This is a traditional cake from Siena in Italy. Serve it in thin wedges to display the nuts and fruit inside.

500g nuts, roughly chopped - any mix of almonds, hazelnuts, brazil nuts or walnuts
500g dried fruit, roughly chopped - include some figs, apricots and apples
¾ cup plain flour
¾ cup chopped chocolate or chocolate chips
½ teaspoon nutmeg
½ teaspoon white pepper
½ teaspoon ground cloves
½ teaspoon ground coriander
1 teaspoon ground cinnamon
160g caster sugar
110g runny honey
2 tablespoons water
cocoa and icing sugar to serve

Pre-heat the oven to 160°C.

Line a 20cm sponge tin with baking paper.

Combine nuts and dried fruit in a bowl with flour, chocolate and spices.

Heat sugar, honey and water in a saucepan, stirring until dissolved.

Bring to the boil and boil for one minute uncovered.

Add the syrup to the fruit and nut mixture and mix well.

Turn the mixture into the prepared tin and pat down evenly.

Bake at 160°C for 30-35 minutes.

Cool the panforte in the tin.

When cool, remove the paper and dust with cocoa and icing sugar combined.

Store wrapped in foil and leave at least one day before cutting.

Panforte stores indefinitely.

cinnamon oysters

This gluten-free recipe has been adapted from a cherished family recipe. The result – the most delectable light sponge kisses flavoured with cinnamon.

2 eggs
4 tablespoons sugar
1 dessertspoon golden syrup
50g rice flour
½ teaspoon cinnamon
½ teaspoon ground ginger
½ teaspoon bicarbonate of soda
whipped cream to serve

Beat the eggs and sugar until thick and then beat in the golden syrup.

Fold in the dry ingredients. Drop spoonfuls of the mixture into greased patty tins and bake for 12 minutes at 190°C.

When cold fill with cream and serve.

the winemakers' autumn feast

There is something about Nelson that creates a sense of it being 'the right place to be'. Take an idyllic physical environment, a most inviting climate, add a vital, creative population and Nelson seems almost too good to be true. It is this sense of perfect lifestyle that has, since the mid 1800's, attracted people who enjoy the good things in life and of course wine has played a part in that enjoyment since Nelson was first settled. German winemakers were among the first settlers in the region, arriving in 1843 and settling in the Upper Moutere area. Although they did not persist with winemaking and many left the area, they left an indelible mark upon the region with many German family and place names.

Over a century later, in the 1960s and 70s a Frenchman, Viggo du Fresne, was determined to make wine in the region. After plenty of trial and error he settled on an offering of robust dry reds from his tiny Ruby Bay vineyard. One of du Fresne's most supportive friends and customers was Toss Woollaston, thus creating an early link between Nelson's wine makers and artists. While du Fresne was among the first of the modern era of winemakers in the region it wasn't until Hermann and Agnes Seifried established vineyards at Upper Moutere in 1974, quickly followed by Craig Gass with Korepo wines and Tim and Judy Finn at Neudorf, that Nelson could be said to be a wine producing area.

To help sell their product and provide an experience that would entice customers back, Korepo Wines (latterly Ruby Bay wines) and Neudorf Vineyards added food to the wine list. It did not take long for visitors and locals alike to embrace the delights offered; in fact food at Neudorf became so popular the Finns were forced to make the choice between being winemakers and restaurateurs. There was never really any question that wine would win over food but the special place that Neudorf Vineyards had quickly become meant there would always be food associated with the wine at Neudorf. While restaurants offered BYO wine Neudorf offered BYO food and this beautiful setting was quickly established as one of the most popular picnic places in the region.

As Nelson moved rapidly into a modern winemaking era the pioneers were joined by an increasing number of grape growers and winemakers. There wasn't a boom in the industry like that seen in Marlborough but growth was steady and strong with a particular emphasis on Riesling, Chardonnay and Pinot Noir. In the mid 1990s Trevor Bolitho started to move from growing apples to grapes and producing wines under the Waimea Estates label, and Phil Jones established the Tasman Bay label. Suddenly Nelson could boast winemakers of considerable size as well as considerable quality. Whilst Seifried, Waimea Estates and Tasman Bay have been particularly successful as producers of high quality, affordable wines the local industry has been underpinned by several exceptional boutique producers. Neudorf Vineyards has established a firm reputation as one of New Zealand's top producers with a range of stunning wines and in recent years they have increased production to levels putting them well above boutique production. Neudorf Vineyards' Moutere Chardonnay is rightly considered a world class, iconic New Zealand wine. On the Waimea Plains Andrew Greenhough and Jenny Wheeler of Greenhough Vineyards established a brand that would quickly become synonymous with the word 'quality'. Greenhough Vineyards produce a range of wines that are a true expression of their growing environment (*terroir*) and their Pinot Noir is among the best in New Zealand.

Winemaking in Nelson is based around two sub-regions with the majority of vines on the flat silty Waimea Plains but with substantial plantings in the Moutere Hills area. Whilst the flat plains are attractive to large scale growers the flavours produced in these vineyards are quite different to those produced in the clay soils of the Moutere Hills. Growers are now expanding into areas north of Nelson City and west into Golden Bay. Early production from vineyards in these new areas shows promise of great things to come. Wine making always has its characters and in Nelson Dave Glover, who established Glover's Vineyards, embodies the spirit of pioneering winemaking. Anyone who has a PhD in algebra has to be just a wee bit eccentric and when the doctor became a winemaker the result was always going to be one of no compromise. Glover has a number plate on his vehicle that reads 'TANNIN' and his range of sturdy reds have tannin in bucket loads. The Dave Glover approach to winemaking is that good things take time and he produces wines that are designed to be aged.

In the early 1990's Seifried Estate made the move from small scale plantings in the Moutere Hills to large scale plantings on the Waimea Plains and their original vineyard and winery was purchased by Greg and Amanda Day and renamed Kahurangi Estate after the Kahurangi National Park. The Days have stamped their own mark on this vineyard that has a special place in the history of modern winemaking in Nelson. While they have expanded the plantings in the area close to the Upper Moutere site they have also had the benefit of some of the pioneering work the Seifrieds did in the early 1970's and have some of the oldest Riesling vines in the South Island. Tucked in the valley behind Kahurangi Estate is the seductive environment of Moutere Hills Wines, another winery where the atmosphere created by a secluded location, good wine and fine food is something rather special. Flesh this out with some live music and it is very easy to while away many sunny Sunday afternoons.

As the industry has matured the key varieties of Chardonnay, Riesling, Sauvignon Blanc and Pinot Noir still form the basis of Nelson wine production. The majority of growth in recent years has taken place on the Waimea Plains with Seifried Estate and Waimea Estates establishing substantial new plantings. Many hectares of vines have been planted by contract growers, some of whom now produce wines under their own label, the most notable among this group being Brightwater Estate. Gary and Valley

Neale were very successful contract growers; their meticulous vineyard management producing fruit that winemakers would die for. Their attention to detail is now being used to produce a range of fruit driven wines bursting with Nelson sunshine.

Nelson is also home to two organic wine producers – Sunset Valley Vineyards and Richmond Plains are both fully certified Bio-Gro producers. Sunset Valley Vineyards are located in the Moutere Hills growing region while Richmond Plains are in the Waimea valley. The wines delivered by these growers reflect sub-regional differences while also displaying typical Nelson ripe fruit characters in their wines. Te Mania Estate's Three Brothers blend was so named when the three Harrey brothers were together one Christmas and it seemed natural that a wine made from the three classic varieties of Cabernet Sauvignon, Cabernet Franc and Merlot be named accordingly. Located on the Waimea Plains, Te Mania has a microclimate that seems perfectly suited to these grape varieties that can be difficult to ripen in other parts of the region.

One producer that has moved from the plains to the hills is Woollaston Estates Philip Woollaston, former MP and mayor of Nelson, is the son of the late Sir Tosswill Woollaston, one of New Zealand's most eminent artists. Philip and wife Chan established Wai-iti River Vineyards at Brightwater before partnering with businessman Glenn Schaeffer and moving to the Moutere Hills to establish about 50 hectares of vineyards, a state of the art winemaking facility and a tasting venue that includes a gallery dedicated to the works of Toss Woollaston. The original Wai-iti vineyard has been taken over by another plains producer, Kaimira Wines. June Hamilton and Ian Miller established Kaimira Wines on the site of an old orchard that was also the site of an early flour mill. Sourcing fruit from their own vineyards and from contract growers throughout the region Kaimira produce a range of wines that show the best of different growing environments in the region.

In the modern era of winemaking in Nelson it has become important for the industry to join together to enhance the region's position in both the local and international market place. As a first step the brand 'Wine Art – fine wine from Nelson' was adopted by the region's wineries. A logical partnership has been established with The Bishop Suter Art Gallery and a lot more will be seen of this marketing brand in years to come.

The photographs here capture an elegant vineyard lunch when Nelson winemakers gathered to celebrate the harvest, bringing some of their favourite recipes to share.

Neil Hodgson

gougere

These cheesy puffs originate from Burgundy and are traditionally served alongside Pinot Noir. They freeze well.

1 cup water
70g butter
1½ teaspoons salt
1½ cups flour

4 eggs (size 6)
125g tasty blue cheese, eg Kikorangi
chopped into small pieces

Combine the water, butter and salt in a saucepan and bring to the boil.

Remove from the heat, add the flour all at once and beat with an electric mixer until the mixture forms a smooth ball.

Place the bottom of the saucepan in cold water for a minute to cool the mixture slightly. Add the eggs one at a time, beating well between each addition until the dough looks glossy and smooth. Beat three quarters of the cheese into the mixture.

Line two oven trays with baking paper and drop teaspoons of the mixture onto them. Top with the remaining cheese.

Bake at 230ºC for five minutes and then reduce the temperature to 180º and bake for 15-20 minutes more.

The gougere should be slightly moist inside. They can be made ahead of time, frozen and reheated.

flax pear and blue cheese rolls

This new take on pear and blue cheese salad was contributed by the chef at Flax Restaurant on Mapua wharf. Ingredients can be varied to use what is in season, to create different flavour and colour combinations, styles and wine matches.

The quantity of each ingredient depends on the number to be served and your own creativity. Nelson Pinot Gris, with its lovely pear and quince flavours, is fantastic served with these rolls.

pears
prosciutto
Kapiti Kikorangi cheese cut in strips
fresh rocket

red capsicum
balsamic vinegar
Nelson olive oil
salt and pepper

Peel and core the pears, cut them into thin wedges, brush with a little olive oil and roast for ten minutes in a hot oven.

Meanwhile, lay out a sushi mat and cover it with cling film. Cover the sushi mat with strips of prosciutto, overlapping them to form a continuous layer.

Next lay out a line of the blue cheese strips, the fresh rocket leaves, the roasted pear wedges and the capsicum.

Roll up the prosciutto tightly as for sushi and refrigerate for an hour.

To make the dressing put balsamic vinegar and olive oil (in the proportion ⅓ to ⅔) into a jar, add salt and pepper to taste, and shake well.

Just before serving cut the rolls into two cm thick slices and remove cling film.

Arrange the rolls on a serving plate and drizzle the dressing over them.

rough island wild duck terrine

Hunting and shooting are popular weekend activities around Nelson, and manuka maimais (duck shooters' hides) are a familiar sight in the Waimea Estuary. This recipe is usually made with paradise duck but any wild duck could be used. Farmed duck just isn't the same! Pinot Noir loves wild foods like duck and rabbit and Nelson produces some beautiful Pinots. Try them with mushrooms and lamb as well.

2 wild duck breasts
3 tablespoons brandy, port or sherry
½ teaspoon allspice
1 onion, chopped
1 tablespoon butter
2 chicken breasts, minced or finely chopped
500g pork, minced or finely chopped

250g pork fat, minced or finely chopped
salt and pepper to taste
2 cloves garlic
½ teaspoon thyme
additional ¼ teaspoon allspice
1 egg, beaten
approximately 10 slices bacon

Slice the duck breast finely and marinate in the brandy mixed with the allspice whilst preparing the other ingredients. Any scraps of duck may be added to the minced meats. Fry the onion in the butter until translucent.

Put the chicken, pork mince, pork fat and onions into a large mixing bowl.

Add the salt, pepper, crushed garlic, thyme, another pinch of allspice and the egg.

Drain the marinade from the sliced duck into the meat mixture and mix well.

Line a terrine or loaf tin with bacon leaving enough at the top edges to pull over the top of the terrine mix.

Press layers of the meat mixture into the terrine alternating with layers of marinated duck strips, finishing with the meat mix. Press down firmly to remove any air pockets.

Fold the bacon over the top of the meat and cover tightly with foil.

Put a lid on the terrine and place in a baking pan with hot water that comes two thirds of the way up the sides of the terrine.

Cook at 180°C for an hour. Remove the terrine from the oven.

Take off the lid and weight the top of the terrine with a brick or heavy cans (cat food cans are ideal). Leave to cool. Like most terrines, the flavours develop so it is best made ahead of time.

devil's thumb venison salad

Nelson abounds in good venison, from wild red deer in the mountains to their fat farmed friends on the plains. If your family lacks a hunter, any gourmet butcher should have venison.

half a venison fillet or backsteak
freshly ground black pepper
rock salt
½ cup olive oil
2-3 teaspoons dark soy sauce
½ fresh or dried chilli, deseeded and finely chopped
1 clove garlic, finely chopped
white base of 2 stalks lemon grass, finely chopped
2 teaspoons fish sauce

juice of one fresh lime or lemon
4 tablespoons salad oil (a mild oil such as canola, soy or corn oil is best)
assorted seasonal salad greens including some fresh chopped coriander and basil leaves
2 spring onions, chopped
other salad ingredients to taste - cucumber, cherry tomatoes, avocado, lightly cooked green beans and grated carrot all work well

Trim the meat, roll it in pepper and salt and smother with the olive oil mixed with the soy sauce. Cover and leave for at least two hours, turning occasionally.

Place the chilli, garlic, lemon grass, fish sauce, lime or lemon juice and oil in a screw top jar and shake well.

Sear the meat over a very hot charcoal barbecue, turning frequently, until a 'well done' crust forms, then wrap in double aluminium foil making a sealed package.

Return to the heat for five minutes, turning again to heat all sides.

Remove from the heat and allow to stand for 20 minutes or until ready to serve.

Just before serving remove the meat from its wrapper, being careful to retain the juices in the foil.

Spread the salad ingredients over a large serving platter.

Slice the meat thinly, place on top of the salad and pour the juices from the foil over the meat. Drizzle the dressing over both meat and salad.

vineyard vegetable tower with pancetta and fresh field mushrooms

This recipe (which serves four) sounds complicated but is actually simple, spectacular and delicious. It is best served with barbecued leg of lamb or grilled breast of chicken. Try adding grilled aubergine slices and chillies to the rosemary stalk for an extra zing. Nelson Sauvignon Blanc is excellent with most vegetable dishes. It is also great with fetta, olives, sun-dried tomatoes and other picnic fare.

3 medium kumara
2 tablespoons olive oil
salt and pepper to taste
peanut oil for frying
8 pancetta rounds
2 large red capsicums
3 tablespoons extra virgin olive oil
8 large flat field mushrooms
2 tablespoons fresh thyme leaves, stripped from the stalks

2 garlic cloves, bruised and chopped
2 tablespoons pink peppercorns, well crushed
1 tablespoon balsamic vinegar
16 baby spinach leaves, washed and blanched in boiling water
4 rosemary twigs stripped of the bottom leaves, for spearing

To cook the rosti: peel and grate the kumara, squeezing out all excess moisture.

Mix the kumara with the oil, salt and pepper and press well together.

Heat a little peanut oil in a heavy bottomed frying pan and fry spoonfuls of the kumara mixture over a moderate heat, making sure that each rosti is well flattened to about the same size as the mushrooms, or a little larger (you will need eight rosti). Drain the rosti on paper towels, place them on a metal tray lined with baking paper and set aside. This can be done several hours ahead of time.

Lay the slices of pancetta in a single layer on another tray lined with one sheet of baking paper and cover with another sheet.

Bake at 180°C until crisp and set to one side.

Cut the capsicums in half, remove the seeds and ribs, brush them with oil and roast in the oven at 200°C until the skins are starting to blacken.

Meanwhile trim the mushrooms and wipe them with a damp paper towel.

Combine thyme leaves with garlic, pink peppercorns, the remaining olive oil and the balsamic vinegar in a bowl.

Add the mushrooms, turning them to coat well, then place into a roasting dish and cook for 12-15 minutes in the oven with the capsicums.

Place the pre-cooked rosti on a separate tray in the oven for the last five minutes of the cooking time.

To assemble the towers, place one re-heated kumara rosti on each plate. Top with one mushroom, four spinach leaves, half a roasted capsicum and another mushroom.

Place two pancetta rounds on top and finish with another kumara rosti.

Spear each tower from top to bottom with a rosemary stalk, leaving a few leaves showing at the top, and drizzle the roasting juice over the whole.

quince and pears in verjuice

To complement this dish look for one of Nelson's beautiful botrytised, late harvest or ice wines - usually Riesling or Gewurztraminer. Those luscious fruit flavours will bring out the ginger notes in this sumptuous dessert.

Verjuice is unfermented grape juice made from the unripe grapes thinned before harvest. It is less acid than lemon juice and can be used in vinaigrettes, for poaching chicken, for deglazing and it is delicious with soda water and ice cubes as a refreshing drink.

4 knobs preserved ginger, chopped
2 tablespoons syrup from ginger
500ml verjuice
2 tablespoons brown sugar

2 quinces, peeled and sliced
2 pears, peeled and quartered
1 cup mascarpone or cream plus extra preserved ginger to serve

Drain the ginger and finely chop it, reserving the syrup. Heat the verjuice and add the ginger, syrup and sugar. Bring to the boil and add the quinces and pears.

Taste and add a little more sugar if you have a sweet tooth.

Poach gently until the quinces are tender when tested with a skewer (about 10 minutes, depending on the variety).

Take the fruit out carefully with a slotted spoon.

Add more chopped ginger and syrup to taste.

Serve at room temperature with slices of homemade gingerbread and whipped cream or mascarpone.

homemade gingerbread

Always a favourite whether served with the quince and pears or on its own fresh from the oven.

2½ cups flour
3 teaspoons baking powder
1 teaspoon baking soda
1 tablespoon ground ginger
1 teaspoon ground cinnamon
pinch of salt

125g butter
½ cup brown sugar
½ cup golden syrup
⅔ cup milk
2 eggs, beaten

Sift the flour, baking powder, baking soda, ginger, cinnamon and salt into a large mixing bowl. Melt the butter, sugar and golden syrup together, add the milk and leave to cool slightly.

Add the beaten eggs and butter mixture to the flour etc and mix well.

Turn into a greased and floured 20 cm square tin and bake at 180ºC for 35-40 minutes. Cool the gingerbread in the tin.

picnic at the lake

In the beginning every meal was a picnic. Middens from fishing camps at Tahunanui indicate Nelson's most famous beach has been a favourite picnic spot since around 1300 AD, while inland at Lake Rotoiti the tuna (eels) were eaten by early Maori along with freshwater mussels that grow in the very cold water of the high altitude lake. The cold water also nurtures the eels; they are the oldest in New Zealand, reaching maturity at about 90 years. Now protected, they were barbecued for Thomas Brunner by his Maori guide Kehu on the outward leg of their epic 19 month exploration of the West Coast in the 1840s. 'In the morning when we awoke, four fine eels were roasting for breakfast and another four were hanging from an adjacent tree', Brunner wrote in the *Nelson Examiner*.

Cooking on a fire and eating in the outdoors is still a way of life for many people around the world. As westerners have moved from a nomadic lifestyle to a settled one and thence to very complex and sophisticated ways of preparing food and taking shelter, the attraction of a simple meal, eaten outside - possibly even prepared over an open fire - has developed its own allure, and Lake Rotoiti remains an ideal place to enact this ritual.

It is actually the French who claim the word *picquenique* as a celebratory outdoor meal, immortalised by Monet in his famous and originally controversial painting of naked diners lunching on the grass. In New Zealand we have evolved our own style of picnic, based on our easy access to, and our love of, the New Zealand coastline, the lake shore, the river bank and the mountain stream. Early settlers perfected the art of camp oven bread, and billy tea became a byword for colonial hospitality. Our picnics also have strong links with sports events, from the pie and thermos at a country rugby match to the more urbane bubbles and club sandwiches from the car boot at the races. Throw that wartime symbol of Kiwi innovation, the Bengazi burner into the mix and you have the sense of improvisation, of being at home in the rugged outdoors, that makes the Kiwi picnic such a cultural icon.

The Kiwi picnic also makes a natural partner to a peculiarly Nelson outdoor event, the annual Seresin Estate Antique and Classic Boat Show. Throw out any notions you have of boat shows run by and for noisy petrol heads or polished teak snobs. Nelson events organiser Pete Rainey is the man behind this show and he gives it a compelling sense of local history. Pete's own links with Rotoiti date from his grandfather's rabbit shooting expeditions, when they travelled to the Lake by train and bicycle. The next generation (Pete's parents) bought a bach at the St Arnaud township in the mid 1960s – originally clad with kerosene tins, it has since been rebuilt. Pete recalls watching the classic speedboat *La Paloma* (Spanish for 'pigeon') cruising past when he was a youngster playing down at the foreshore in the family dinghy. In those days he thought it was 'really old fashioned', but he has changed his view of the classic craft since he bought and restored it ready for the 2003 Boat Show.

Part of the Boat Show's charm is that it doesn't take itself too seriously – it has a strong sense of the absurd. Even the boat owners are willing to admit it is a little crazy to hunt down old clinkers abandoned in sheds and to spend years tracing boat history and sanding and polishing boat bits. The end result is a show that delivers the unusual all round: a dinghy that saw Dunkirk, another bought from Te Rauparaha's descendents on Kapiti Island, a 'race' for the slowest rowing boat, and an overall winner who shouts 'Long live steam!' as he holds his trophy aloft.

The Boat Show at Lake Rotoiti was first held in 2000, but it has its origins way back in the history of this alpine village in the Nelson Lakes National Park. In the early days of European settlement, the trip from Nelson to Marlborough was either by boat, or by horse transport via the Lake. Tophouse was a well-known stopping point and the original building is still in the hospitality business. In 1855 a Scottish settler, John Kerr, took up the Lake Run and, alongside his farming interests, nurtured his love for boats and fishing. In 1873 he bought 500 brown trout ova from the Nelson Acclimatisation Society and released them into the Black Valley Stream – where the trout still return annually to spawn.

Boating at the Lake has been a popular pastime for Nelsonians for generations, with a record from 1880 of a church party taking a dinghy up for a week's holiday. The first power boat race in the 1920s drew just two competitors, the *Eileen* and the *.303*, racing for a condensed milk can with handles soldered on and the name of the winner scratched into the tin. A far cry from the sleek Jens Hansen silver trophy of today! Names of boats such as *Fleetwing* and *No Catchem* (which was also an earlier name for the St Arnaud Range) are still bandied about by old timers. From 1926 boat races were held on New Year's Day and Easter Monday, progressing over the years from whalers with three hp motors to the memorable battles between the Ford V8 hydroplanes *Lady Luck* and *Flak* of the late '40s.

It is these boats, their working predecessors and streamlined replicas of traditional craft, that are celebrated annually on the first weekend in March at the Seresin Estate Antique and Classic Boat Show. With over 100 boats and 2000 onlookers there is a crowded beach for the 'Le Mans' start of the Seagull race. Picture it: a row of rocking dinghies, a mass man-versus-motor tussle, the relief as starter cords entice action from these old fashioned outboard motors – and mortification for those left behind. Boats are the stars of this show and, inevitably, many come with their own stories. The philosophy of this type of boat ownership and restoration is closely akin to the philosophy of the Kiwi picnic. Backyard boat-building is the last frontier of the Kiwi Do It Yourself ethic according to Ian Walker who uses his squarish dinghy, aptly named *Pointless*, for flounder netting in the Pelorus Sound. He notes that the Building Code has stifled innovation on baches and even sheds, but with boats you can still build whatever you like. *Pointless* is from the stable of eccentric Massachusetts designer Phil Bolger, who set out to create a vessel giving the maximum loading possible from three sheets of marine ply. An inscription on the hull states that *Pointless* will take four men and one frightened dog.

Pretty in pink is *Pandora*, a working boat launched in 1935. Designed and built by A.S. 'Porkie' King Turner who fished the outer Sounds, from his home in Ketu Bay to Stephens Island, French Pass, the Chetwodes and Forsyth. It was not unusual for *Pandora* to carry up to a tonne of fish plus her fishing gear, and Porkie was skilled at getting her home with a mere two inches of freeboard. *Pandora* is now enjoying a stylish retirement; restored by Vic King Turner, Porkie's son, who has gathered up a collection of cotton set nets, cod hand lines, willow craypots and a hemp anchor rope to fit out the boat.

While the world rushes into the 21st century, antique and classic boat owners are taking a step back to share a day out at the Lake, a boat race or two, and a picnic lunch that (like the old boats) is streamlined, simple, and rich with heritage. The menu for the Boat Show picnic is suitably masculine and hearty: boating is physical and the weather at the Lake can be chilly. The onion soup is in the French tradition, but the puffy little cheese meringue croutons provide a fresh touch. Barley water is a long time favourite summer drink, and travels well as a cordial and the picnic is rounded off richly with Olive's baked fruitcake. The style of fruit can be varied with more prunes and figs if it is to be used as a pudding, more currants and sultanas if it is to go in a lunch box. Enjoy Olive's legacy with a brew of billy tea enlivened with a dash of whisky.

Jacquetta Bell

boaties' brew

Billy tea is a tradition in the outdoor wilderness areas of New Zealand, and can be made by hanging a billy of water over a campfire or lighting up the thermette.

Fire up the thermette, and bring the water to the boil. Pour into the heated billy, and add the leaf tea allowing one teaspoon for each person. Allow tea to brew.
Pour the steaming tea into mugs, adding rich bush honey and nips of whisky to taste.

lemon and barley water

Lemon and barley water is a refreshing drink for hot summer days, and many rural New Zealanders will remember walking long distances to the back paddocks of the farm to deliver a billy of lemon and barley water and other treats to family and farm workers during haymaking.

½ cup pearl barley   ½ cup sugar
zest of two lemons   200ml lemon juice

Rinse barley well, cover with plenty of water and bring to the boil for three minutes.
Drain, refresh with more water and return to the pan.
Pour on one litre of cold water, add lemon zest, and bring to a rolling boil. Cover and simmer for 20 minutes. Sieve out barley from remaining liquid.
Stir in sugar and leave until cold. Add lemon juice and bottle.
To serve, treat as a cordial adding ice cubes, water and lemon slices to each glass.

rotoiti rainbow eggs

Scotch eggs are a well-known picnic treat. Here they get a vegetarian twist which makes them quite special. When sliced they show splashes of red (from the capsicum) and green (from the spinach).

1 medium onion, finely chopped
2 cloves garlic, crushed
1 tablespoon olive oil
¾ cup chick peas, cooked and drained
(or use 1 400g can cooked chick peas)
1 teaspoon dry mustard
1½ teaspoons cumin (more if you like it)
½ cup parsley, chopped
¼ cup smooth peanut butter
¼ teaspoon celery salt
1 teaspoon paprika
½ teaspoon freshly ground pepper
1 teaspoon salt
juice of 1 lemon
½ cup plain unsweetened yoghurt
1 tablespoon Worcestershire sauce
1 roasted red capsicum, chopped
1 large handful spinach leaves, blanched, drained and chopped
6 hard boiled eggs
1 cup breadcrumbs

Cook the onion and garlic in the olive oil until translucent.
Chop the chick peas in the food processor.
Add the mustard, cumin, parsley, peanut butter, celery salt, paprika, pepper, salt, lemon juice, yoghurt and Worcestershire sauce and pulse briefly.
Turn into a mixing bowl and stir in the onions and garlic, the capsicum and the spinach.
The mixture should just hold its shape. If it is too wet add a little wholemeal flour; if it is too dry add a little more lemon juice.
Now cover the eggs with the chick pea mixture. For each egg spread about half a cup of mixture on your palm, place the egg on top and pat the mixture around the egg until it is firm.
Roll each egg in breadcrumbs and place on a greased baking sheet.
Bake at 220°C until the crumbs are firm and lightly browned.

mt robert onion soup with meringue croutons

This soup is a great warmer for boating or skiing in the clear alpine air of the Nelson Lakes National Park, and is easily transported in a thermos flask. The croutons add a light crunch to the soft, sweet soup.

1kg onions, thinly sliced
3 cloves garlic, crushed
2 tablespoons brown sugar
2 tablespoons butter
2 litres good chicken or beef stock
½ cup tomato puree
2 cups red or white wine

2 tablespoons Worcestershire sauce
2 tablespoons cornflour
½ cup sherry
1 tablespoon sherry vinegar
salt and pepper
250g shallots, thinly sliced

Cook onions, garlic, brown sugar and butter together slowly until caramelised and soft.
Add stock, tomato puree, wine and Worcestershire sauce.
Simmer for 30 minutes. Remove from heat. Mix cornflour with sherry and add slowly to soup, stirring constantly.
Bring to the boil and simmer for ten minutes.
Add sherry vinegar and salt and pepper to taste.
Serve soup with croutons and shallots fried until crisp.

Croutons

3 egg whites
1 teaspoon cream of tartar
pinch of salt

1 handful freshly grated Parmesan cheese

Whisk egg whites to soft peaks with cream of tartar and salt. Gently fold in Parmesan cheese. Drop spoonfuls onto a baking tray and place into a hot oven. Turn heat to low and bake until crisp.

smoked eel paté

Fresh water eels were known as 'tuna' by the early Maori and were traditionally cooked over an open fire. If you are able to access fresh eels, the smaller ones make better eating than the very large, and they can be skinned and cooked in a fish smoker. However, many supermarkets now stock smoked eel which is perfectly adequate in this recipe.

400g smoked eel fillets
1 large onion, finely diced
5 cloves garlic, minced
70g butter
2 tablespoons coarsely chopped thyme, marjoram and flat leaf parsley

sea salt
freshly ground pepper
olive oil
fresh brown bread

Remove any skin from the eel fillets.
Sauté the onion and garlic in the butter over low heat until lightly golden – approximately 15–20 minutes. Remove from the heat.
Coarsely flake the eel fillets and mix with the warm onions and garlic.
Season with fresh herbs, sea salt and freshly ground pepper to taste.
Press into a lightly oiled dish and serve warm or cold with fresh brown bread.

no catchem venison and mushroom terrine

Wild venison is used in this recipe and the marinade moderates the 'gamy' taste. Farmed venison is also a fine choice for this tasty picnic fare.

500g venison, roughly chopped
1 thick slice white bread
300g bacon (preferably butcher's bacon not skinny little bits of packaged bacon)
1 onion finely chopped
2-3 shallots (optional)
1 tablespoon flour
1 egg, beaten
3 teaspoons salt (it seems a lot but it needs it)

1 teaspoon freshly ground pepper
1 teaspoon dried thyme
½ teaspoon ground savoury
½ teaspoon ground cloves
200g Portobello mushrooms
4-6 rashers extra bacon to line the terrine
sage leaves to garnish

Marinade

I carrot, finely chopped
I shallot, finely chopped
1 tablespoon olive oil
240m (drinkable!) red wine

½ teaspoon salt
parsley, fresh thyme, a bay leaf and a handful of sage leaves

First prepare the marinade: lightly fry carrot and shallot in the oil, add remainder of marinade ingredients and simmer gently for 10 minutes. Set aside to cool.

Add the chopped venison, cover with plastic wrap and place in the refrigerator for 24 hours. Drain the venison (reserving the liquid) and soak the bread in the marinade.

Put the venison, bacon, onion and shallot into a food processor and chop.

Add the flour, egg, salt, pepper, herbs and cloves and mix again. Add the bread and pulse. Leave to stand for 10-20 minutes.

Add the mushrooms and lightly pulse. Line a terrine or loaf tin with bacon. Press in the verison mixture and cover with more bacon. Add some sage leaves to the top for decoration. Put on a lid (or cover with foil) and bake in a roasting dish half full of water at 160°C for 90 minutes. Leave terrine to cool, and store in the refrigerator for a day or two to bring out a richer flavour.

green salad with lime vinaigrette

Fresh limes and spices add zest to this crunchy salad.

1 buttercrunch lettuce
handful of fresh watercress

assorted other leaf greens – cos or iceberg lettuce, baby spinach etc

Wash and dry the greens and put in a salad bowl. Shake the vinaigrette and pour over the greens just before serving.

Lime vinaigrette

juice and grated zest of two limes
1 tablespoon verjuice or light vinegar
125ml light olive oil
½ teaspoon Szechwan peppercorns, crushed

¼ tablespoon ground cardamom
pinch ground cumin seed
salt and pepper to taste

Shake all ingredients together in a jar, adding more olive oil if the dressing is too sharp. Lime vinaigrette is also delicious used as a marinade for scallops or prawns.

olive's baked fruitcake

This fruitcake came from a recipe book that was left behind in a Westport house. The house had a coal range, which is the very best way to cook this cake. The style of fruit can be varied, more prunes and figs if it is to be used as a pudding, more currants and sultanas if it is to go in a lunch box. Olive's legacy is this baked fruitcake.

1kg chopped dried fruit - figs, prunes, apricots etc
1½ cups water
125g butter
1½ cups sugar

2 cups flour
1 teaspoon baking powder
2 eggs, beaten
½ cup blanched almonds

Simmer fruit with water, butter and sugar for ten minutes. Cool, and stir in flour, baking powder and eggs. Turn into a greased and floured cake tin and dot the top with blanched almonds. Bake in a moderate oven for approximately one hour or until a knife comes out clean. For a picnic cut slices, lightly butter both sides and toast in a hot pan over the *thermette* ring. Serve immediately with a wedge of Kikorangi blue cheese and a spoonful of pickled plums.

pickled plums
(with olive's baked fruit cake)

The sugar in this recipe can be adjusted depending on whether you like a sharp tang to your pickles or a more mellow flavour.

600ml cider or white vinegar
add your favourite spice - a couple of cinnamon sticks, some whole cloves, a few cardamom pods, or vanilla beans

1kg sugar
2kg plums

Bring the vinegar and spices to the boil and add the sugar.
Boil for a couple of minutes before adding the plums.
Simmer for just a few minutes and bottle.
The juice around the plums can be used in all sorts of sweet and savoury dishes. Add to ice cream, drizzle it over slices of warm duck, use it to lift the flavour in casseroles, or serve it over blue cheese with toasted slices of Olive's fruitcake for a picnic.

glossary

bach — a simple house or cottage, often at the beach, used on weekends or holidays

beach seine — a fishing net with floats at the top and weights at the bottom used to encircle fish and haul them ashore

beanie — a small close-fitting hat

Benghazi burner — an early name for a thermette or similar water boiler

billy — a cooking pot with a lid and wire handle used over a camp fire

BYO — bring your own, as in 'bring your own drinks' etc

camp oven — a heavy iron cooking pot usually used over a camp fire

chilly bin — a portable insulated container for keeping food or drink cool

cockle — *Austrovenus stutchburyi*, a small bivalve shellfish

croquembouche — a conical cake made from cream-filled balls of choux pastry

falafel — spicy patties made from crushed chick peas or beans

ganache — a rich chocolate mixture containing cream and/or butter

GDP — gross domestic product; the value of all goods produced and services provided in an economy in one year

geoduck clam — *Panopea zelandica*, a New Zealand shellfish

julienne — to cut vegetables into narrow strips about the size of matchsticks

jus — a sauce consisting primarily of the cooking juices of meat

kaharoa — seine net or large drag net

kai moana — seafood

kaka — *Nestor meridionalis*, a large New Zealand parrot

kereru — *Hemiphaga novaeseelandiae*, the New Zealand wood pigeon

kiwi — any of the New Zealand species of the genus *Apteryx*; a flightless, nocturnal bird. *Kiwi* is also a colloquial term for a New Zealander.

leatherjacket — a name given to various marine fish with a leathery skin

lolly — a piece of confectionary, usually a boiled sweet or toffee

long drop — a hole in the ground used as an outside toilet (usually enclosed in a rough shed-like structure)

mahi-mahi — *Coryphaena hippurus*, a blue and silver marine fish

maimai — a duck shooter's hide

manuka — *Leptospermum scoparium*; a small New Zealand tree with aromatic leaves

Mouli — a kitchen implement used for sieving cooked food (often vegetables) for soups etc

oast house — a building containing a kiln for drying hops

otter trawl — the name originally given to a trawl net which was fitted with otter doors on either side of the mouth of the net. As the net was drawn through the water, the flow of water over the doors increased the horizontal opening of the net.

pa — a Maori village

Pakeha — a white-skinned person, usually of European ancestry

paua — *Haliotis iris*, a member of the abalone family

peck — an imperial measure for dry goods which is equivalent to 7.57 litres

pipi — *Paphies australis*, a small bivalve shellfish

plum duff — a pudding made with dried fruit, especially sultanas or currants

safe — a cabinet for keeping meat and other perishable foods

sea lettuce — *Ulva lactula*, a shallow water seaweed with green fronds which resemble lettuce

Szechwan peppercorns — the seeds of *Xanthoxylum piperitum*, which have a spicy and distinctive flavour unlike true pepper

tapu — sacred or forbidden for religious reasons

thermette — a cylindrical container for heating water outdoors, which has a hollow centre for adding small pieces of wood etc. to a fire lit in its base

tuatua — *Paphies subtriangulata* or *P. donacina*, two species of edible New Zealand shellfish

ute — a utility vehicle or small truck

waka — a receptacle, box, Maori canoe, etc

warehou — *Seriolella brama*, a firm-fleshed, middle depth fish species

recipe index

acknowledgements

The production team extend their thanks to the recipe contributors and the many other individuals and businesses in the Nelson community who have given so generously of their time, produce, and expertise to support *The Outside Table* as a fundraising venture for the redevelopment of The Bishop Suter Art Gallery.

Foreword Sir Patrick Goodman, PCNZM, Kt.Bach., CBE

Introduction David Burton

Beach Cook-up at Wainui Bay Linda Walker, Stéphane Cornille, Zénobie Cornille, Robin King, Nigel Peterson, Anne Rush, Barry Walker, Claudia Walker, Deborah Walsh, Paul Winspear.

A Magical Celebration Deborah Walsh, Sue Bevin, Tony Duncan, Porche Duncan, Anthony Fawcett, Steve Fullmer, Christine Johnston, Dee Jones, Joanna Jones, Lucy Jones, Ruby Jones, Poppy and Suzy Kietzman, Ella Minhinnick, Nigel Peterson, Steve Richards, Olivia Russell, Samantha Russell, Steve Russell, Tina Thomas, Judy van Yssel-Richards, Linda Walker, Ju and Judy Yang, Wesley Yang.

When the Boats Come in Alec Woods, Glenys Baldick, Murray Dill, Judy Finn, Donna Hiser, Jenny Gargiulo, Salvi Gargiulo, Michael Lawrence, Rob McKegney, Ellen De Meulemeester, Jane Rose, Anne Rush, Derek Shepherd, Judy Talley, Britannia Antiques, Pomeroy's Coffee and Tea Company, Rosy Glow Chocolates, The Mussel Inn, The Oyster Bar.

Boutique Brews Martin Townshend, Lyn Canton, Alastair Cotterell, John Duncan, Margaret Duncan, Matt Duncan, Rosie Duncan, Sholto Duncan, Pat Edwards, Judy Finn, Donna Hiser, Anne Rush, Barry Walker, Antiquary, Founders Brewery, Founders Historic Park, Lighthouse Brewery, My Pie, Tozzetti Panetteria Ltd.

To Market, to Market Marilyn Andrews, Barbara Raeburn, Eelco Boswijk, Nikki Cantrick, Poppy Dearbourn, Judy Finn, Jill Harris, Mary Heaphy, Jan Heath, John Hicks, Nita Knight, Rachel Kwon, Ricky Kwon, Jennifer Lee, Lois Limmer, Wolfgang Mann, Bill Page, Linda Walker.

Afternoon Tea on the Orchard Anne Rush, Joyanne and Richard Easton, Pat Edwards, Brent Ferretti, Frances Harris, Mary Heaphy, Lois Limmer, Adele Robson, Julie Rowling, Natalie Rush, Sarah Rush, Linda Walker, Candace Wood, Appleby Fresh.

The Winemakers' Autumn Feast Neil Hodgson, Christine Boswijk, Amanda Day, Judy and Tim Finn, Rosie Finn, Steve Fullmer, Dave and Penny Glover, Helen MacGibbon, Heidi Seifried, Agnes and Hermann Seifried, Barbara and Patrick Stow, Andrew and Jenny Wheeler, Chan and Philip Woollaston.

Picnic at the Lake Jacquetta Bell, Owen Bartlett, Pat Edwards, Judy Finn, John Harris, Duncan McFarlane, Pete Rainey, Martin Taylor, Richard Walker, Deborah Walsh, Awaroa Lodge, Seresin Estate Antique and Classic Boat Show.

Design Jo Williams, Nimbus Advertising.

Photography Véronique Cornille, with Daniel Allen (page 80), Alan Doak (page 104), Kevin Judd (pages 10 and 11), Craig Potton (page 44), Grant Stirling (page 95) and Ian Trafford (page 14, image courtesy of Latitude Nelson).

Base map (page 6) GeographX

Proofreading Garry Dickinson, Rosalie Dickinson, Donna Hiser, Ann Nighy, Alison Roxburgh, Anne Rush.

Publishing Support Robbie Burton and Tina Delceg, Craig Potton Publishing, Tordis Flath.

Financial and Marketing Advice Pete Watkins, Ray Wilson.

The Bishop Suter Art Gallery Trust Board and Gallery Director Sari Hodgson, Donna Hiser, Judy Finn, Hugo Judd, Taitamariki Mihaere, David Monopoli, Michael O'Dea, Christopher Watson, Paul Matheson, Elaine Henry, Gabrielle Coote, Helen Telford (Gallery Director).

The Suter 2000 Appeal Trust Sir Patrick Goodman, Royce McGlashen, Alison Roxburgh.

The Suter 2000 Appeal Trust Steering Group Alan Harwood, Jane Evans, Hugo Judd, Taitamariki Mihaere, Russell Poole, Alison Roxburgh, Anne Rush, Helen Telford, Ray Wilson.